YOU'RE NOT CRAZY – YOU'RE CODEPENDENT.

What Everyone Affected By

✓ *Addiction*
✓ *Abuse*
✓ *Trauma*
✓ *Toxic Shaming*

Must Know To Have Peace In Their Lives

Second Edition

By
Jeanette Elisabeth Menter

You're Not Crazy-You're Codependent

J₂
PUBLICATIONS

ISBN-10 0615533469
EAN-13 9780615533469

Dedicated to overcomers everywhere.
May you finally enjoy freedom and peace.
JM

You're Not Crazy-You're Codependent

PREFACE

When I wrote this book almost five years ago, I never imagined it would be used by small groups and individuals in India, Great Britain, Australia, Europe, Japan and Canada as well as all over America. I am continually amazed and disturbed there are so many people on the planet who desperately need this kind of help. Judging by the majority of reviews the book has gotten, it's providing that help effectively.

A lot has changed since its publication. My mother, who I wrote about extensively, passed away from complications of dementia. My husband and I relocated to Las Vegas.

But this book continues to stand on its own as a testimony to what helped me. While not perfect, it is sincere. In this second edition, we have made a few changes and done a little more editing. It's my fervent hope that it will give you the inspiration, courage and knowledge you need to begin the journey into the life you were always meant to have. You deserve that. *Please* do the work. Nothing changes until we get moving. Start today (and remember to finish!).

Jeanette

"I choose to live by faith and not by fear." JM

You're Not Crazy-You're Codependent

INTRODUCTION

"Only the wounded physician heals…and then only to the extent he has healed himself." – Carl Jung

There are two kinds of people who write books like this. The first are the professionals who are experts in their fields and have lots of case histories to share. The second are people who have come to the realization their lives have been consumed by the brokenness and the wrong thinking of their past. These survivors make a decision do whatever it takes to heal from their wounds, overcome them and go on to help others by sharing what they have learned. I am in the second group.

There are no initials after my name. I've just tried to live my life while overcoming the debilitating effects of being raised by an alcoholic father and a neurotic enabling mother, which resulted in all the traits of a codependent being firmly established in my character makeup, which of course, made me feel crazy most of the time. Everything I will put forth to help you is the result of figuring out what worked for me. It still does to this day.

I knew it was the right time to write this book because whenever I came to a place where I felt lost or in need of help, the answers appeared right on time, as if by providence. Over the years I have accumulated quite a collection of books that have helped me on many levels. They were filled with highlighted and bent pages for future reference and put back on the shelf. It was almost mystical how the answers to my questions were found on those very pages as I was drawn to one book or another at the perfect time. *"When the student is ready, the teacher will appear"* was never more true than in this ongoing occurrence. I had unwittingly been preparing myself, with God's help, through the many challenges, years and books I had gone through.

Much of the factual information I provide in my book is a compilation of material from the books I've read. The authors and their works are listed in the Resource section at the end. I'm grateful to all of them. I encourage you to read as much as you can get your hands on. Information is power. The more you acquire the more ammunition you'll have.

This book required complete honesty on my part. It was hard for me to write because my insecure programming kept creeping in and reminding me I'm not an expert. This type of wrong-thinking is an example of why people like you and I have to be aware of what we accept as truth every minute. Also, parts of it are very personal. I'm putting my life on the page for all to see, warts and all. It's an uncomfortable place to be, but necessary. In the end, I realized all I could do is tell what I know is true for me and do it honestly. Even if parts of it feel shameful.

If it's done with the right attitude, this book will be hard for the reader also, but there isn't any other way. Some things as they say cannot be gone around. They must be gone through.

Thank you for letting me share my story and what I've learned along the way. It's very likely you experienced much worse. But as a friend of mine, who is not only a cancer survivor, but one of the happiest people I know in spite of her own history of challenges; once reminded me: pain is pain. There is no hierarchy.

By the way, I used to put books back on the shelf when they required that I write or do something besides read. That decision cost me years of lost time. Don't make the same mistake. Stop wasting time because you do not want to participate in your own healing. Be proactive and do the work. *This is your story. I'm just helping you write it.*

Two items I want to address before we begin:

The first is a concern a couple of readers have had regarding my use of **'religion'** as a tool to heal. As I stress throughout this book, I do not encourage religion. I'm not trying to convert anyone. Rather I talk about the benefits of a relationship with a loving God as one of the pillars to overcoming life's obstacles because that's what works for me and that is all I can write about with certainty. **If you truly do not believe in a higher power, this book may not be for you.**

The second is a housekeeping note. I strongly encourage you to have a journal ready when you read. Although I've left room to make notes, I hope you'll take it upon yourself to go into more depth. You'll see why as you proceed.

If you're using an E-Reader, this is even more important. Your notes are imperative to your progress.

Let's get to work!

"Courage is resistance to fear, mastery of fear not the absence of fear - Mark Twain

TABLE OF CONTENTS

PART ONE

YOU'RE NOT CRAZY

"Although the world is full of suffering,
it is full also of the overcoming of it." – Helen Keller

The pieces of the puzzle

Y ou picked this book up because you are hurting. People

hurt because things have been done to them, whether in the past or in their current situation. Many times we cause our own pain. However it began, it ends up leaving us feeling lost and crazy.

There is a common denominator to much of what we struggle with. It's a big, messy puzzle. Sorting through all the components of your pain requires putting all the pieces of the puzzle on the table. Then we'll begin the process of putting them together so the problem has a face and a name.

Do the following words fit anywhere in your childhood or even a current relationship in which you struggle?

- **Addiction**
- **Abuse**
- **Shame**
- **Trauma**
- **Guilt**
- **Anxiety**

- **Low self esteem**
- **Obsessive behavior**
- **Sexual issues**
- **History of dysfunctional relationships**
- **Anger issues**
- **Care-taking/rescuer personality**
- **Overly responsible or controlling**
- **Depression**

Although this book isn't about any one single issue listed above, it *is* about how they are all connected and how this combination of events and characteristics has created dysfunction in your thinking, behavior and life. Each one takes bravery and persistence to overcome. Maybe you've won the fight against whatever challenges were holding you back, but your thinking and

> **Vital Sign**
> **Being codependent means**
> **you have lost yourself while trying to enable,**
> **fix and control those around you.**

your life is still a mess. That's because these hurdles; especially the first (and primary) ones: addiction, abuse, trauma and shame have created a new, less visible and more complicated problem that lives inside you. This is the crazy-maker because you believed that since you had beat the huge issues you were saddled with that you ought to feel normal, but you don't. Happiness and peace seem to be out of your reach. This inability to feel 'normal' leaves you feeling crazy. Your life is like a puzzle with a piece missing. Here's what you need to know:

You are codependent.

The word codependency is overused, misunderstood and amazingly to me, still unknown to many. It also – in my opinion – is a misleading term. While everyone who has studied it agrees on the characteristics, there are many different opinions on what actually causes or creates a codependent personality. I believe all roads lead back to addiction, abuse, trauma or a shame-based upbringing or relationship.

Several decades ago, it was used to describe a person who was involved with someone else who was dependent (or addicted) to a substance which had taken control of their lives. This person was 'co-dependent' in a sense to the same addict-consumed lifestyle.

Later, it became a more mainstream way to describe anyone who comes from a dysfunctional background where, as a child, the emotional needs are not met. Instead of a healthy environment where she is heard, acknowledged, nurtured, loved; she instead feels ignored, fearful, belittled and responsible for the adult's well-being. In these families, spontaneity and laughter are replaced with rigidness, the inability to engage in honest communication, an abundance of secrets and a proliferation of rules – spoken and unspoken – that all work together to help everyone cope with the tension in the home. Individuals are often enmeshed, meaning they are too entangled in the other's emotions. One person feels responsible for the other. Boundaries are often overlapping or nonexistent. **Addiction is often involved, but not always.** All of this negativity, hostility and emotional confusion make the child scared, insecure and eventually angry. *It is a fact, however, that many people who are struggling with codependency are also saddled with addiction of some kind. The two are deeply* *intertwined in many cases. But this is not a universal scenario. If you are battling addiction, you most likely are also caught up in codependency and may not even know it yet.*

In many cases, physical and sexual abuse are present. This leads to deeper, more dangerous feelings in the child of rage, guilt and shame. Extreme cases can result in children 'splitting' or disassociating. In other words, they mentally check out in order to not feel the unbearable pain of what is happening. Amnesia is common in severe situations.

Messages such as "Don't talk about it," "Don't feel," "It's your job to protect me and keep me happy," or "You're bad," create uncertainty and a sense of 'craziness' and are all common in a dysfunctional environment. These types of messages can also be found in adult relationships which are shame-based.

By the time the child leaves family of origin, all these unhealthy emotions have come together to form the personality of a 'codependent' adult – even if the now adult has no personal chemical dependency. The traits remain because the behavior in a home with addiction and the types of environments a codependent emerges from is essentially the same.

As an adult, these people either consciously or unconsciously seek out partners who continue the patterns of dysfunction he or she was raised with if the wrong thinking is not recognized and changed. They are attracted to addicts, manipulators and abusive or emotionally unavailable people, all of whom continue to mistreat them in the way that seems normal because it is all they understand. They are known for being controlling, insecure people pleasers.

Codependency hasn't officially been classified as a disorder. Many view it as a 'condition' a person takes on as a result of a long term relationship with an unstable, needy or even mentally ill person (such as an addict, or overly protective, domineering and highly controlling parent or partner). This is not a *diagnosis* as much as a *description* of a personality type. Many times, it's a learned behavior picked up by watching others acting out as a result of harm done to them.

Melanie Beattie, author of some of the first books on this subject wrote that many codependents become caretakers and rescuers in the unhealthiest sense. In addition, they suffer from a myriad of other problems, including:

- Low self-worth – resulting in never-ending attempts at people pleasing
- Repression – a fear of speaking up lest there be punishment or rejection
- Obsession – the mind cannot stop ruminating and rationalizing
- Controlling – believes everything is their responsibility to fix
- Denial – don't see that they are the problem
- Dependency – unhealthy attachments creating insecurities
- Poor communication – can't say or don't know what they feel
- Weak boundaries – let others manipulate them

- Lack of trust – can't relax in a relationship; hyper-vigilant
- Anger – unexpressed but constant
- Sex problems – stress levels prevent ability to enjoy; have unwanted sex

She goes on to explain that codependency is a progressive disorder and in time lethargy and depression are not uncommon. Withdrawal and isolation occur. The codependent "may experience a complete loss of daily routine and structure, neglect or abuse their children and other responsibilities, feel hopeless, consider suicide, become violent or develop serious emotional, mental or physical illnesses, develop eating disorders or become addicted to alcohol and other drugs." (*Codependent No More*, 1992).

My own version as a result of what I was raised with can be boiled down to three core beliefs:

1. *My 'happiness' depended on whether or not everyone around me was appeased and approved of me, no matter what it cost in terms of my own well being.*
2. *I was responsible for fixing everyone and their problems.*
3. *I was 'bad' and terrified of rejection.*

The result of all this was I had no idea who I really was or what wanted, but rather saw myself as an extension of whoever it was I was trying to appease.

The root of all codependent characteristics, in my opinion, is the unmet need for approval. In clinical circles, this is also understood to be the basis for attachment disorders which is all about how we relate to other people and why.

Codependency –
the missing piece to having peace

Being codependent will rob you of a real life, leaving you to repeat the behaviors in your past that keep delivering the wrong results. It will distort your view of yourself. It will influence everything you say, every decision you make – your entire path in life will be the unfolding of the effects of being half a person. In addition, you are doomed to pass this legacy of unhappiness on to your children by not stopping the cycle.

If you are tired of relationships that only hurt you, harmful habits, destructive generational patterns, emotional wounds that never go away, feeling powerless to change your thinking and the knowledge your life is just not working, in addition to all the core issues listed earlier, then you must understand codependency. It is the missing piece in your life's puzzle.

Answer these questions "yes" or "no"

1. In your family of origin, was there any sort of addiction? ____

2. Do you often feel frozen or numb?___

3. Was there abuse of any kind? ___

4. Did you feel loved? ___

5. Was continual shaming used to manipulate you? ___

6. Do you have ongoing guilt even when there is no real reason? ___

7. Are you insecure? ___

8. Do you say 'yes' when you want to say 'no'? ___

9. Do you consider yourself to be a caretaker/rescuer? ___

10. Are you in a relationship with someone who has addiction issues? ___

11. Is playing and laughter uncomfortable for you? ___

12. Do you worry excessively? ___

13. Do you find yourself trying to change people around you often? ___

14. Is appearing perfect or just right highly important to you? ___

15. Are you angry most of the time? __

16. Do you find it difficult to make even little decisions?__

17. Do you feel overwhelmed often? ___

18. Do you have a constant feeling of emptiness you can't get rid of? ___
19. Do you struggle with anxiety? ___
20. Are you terrified of rejection or abandonment? ___
21. Do you have ongoing physical problems?____

If you answered "yes" to the majority of these questions, it's no surprise you picked this book up. You are most likely codependent.

This isn't a lifetime sentence, however. There are hundreds of symptoms describing codependency and everybody has some of them sometimes to one degree or another. As with all disorders, it's the degree to which we are steeped in them which takes us from functioning to dysfunctional.

Just as a recovering alcoholic will always be an alcoholic, the codependent, even when he or she has overcome so much of what created the disorder, will from time to time manifest some of the symptoms described previously. That's okay. We aren't struggling to attain perfection here. That's the codependent's fantasy. We are working toward gaining balance in our emotions, thoughts and actions.

Causes and effects

There isn't one single cause or scenario that creates codependency. That's why it's so hard for people to understand it. But when they see certain traits, they relate easily.

There are four issues – or enemies of a healthy life, however, that in my opinion are common threads in codependents' stories. By strange coincidence, each of them shares many of the same characteristics. I have never seen them lined up together in a book about codependency which is why I'm including them here. I believe the connection of all four to how a person becomes codependent is undeniable.

<u>Four most common causes in codependency</u>
<u>personality development</u>
*Addiction
*Abuse
*Trauma
*Shame-based treatment

The role of addiction

Since the word codependency originally emerged as a way to describe a person who was in a relationship with someone dependent on some sort of substance that made their life unmanageable, it has to be the first issue we look at closely because it is so deeply connected with codependency.

My father was an alcoholic. When I talk to others who share codependent traits, there is almost always someone in their family (often multiple people) who struggle with addiction. In some families, it's a generational problem which goes way, way back. I've found that at first many codependents deny addiction was a factor in their family. Upon closer scrutiny, it usually surfaces in some way, somewhere.

Addiction affects the family system in deep, lasting and often unspoken ways.

- **Boundaries** – in a home with addiction, boundaries go from one extreme to another. At one end relationships are enmeshed, meaning individuals are too close, differences are not allowed, over-responsibility for each other exists and there is a loss of self-identity. These are the families in which children are not allowed to pull away. There is no encouragement for the child to pursue talents, interests, etc. In marriages, individuality is given up for the sake of the relationship.

At the other end, relationships are distant with little intimacy. Little sharing of emotion or connectedness occurs and isolation exists from one another. Sometimes the family isolates from the community.

- **Rules** – Again, there are two extremes. Either there is an abundance of rigidness, spoken and unspoken which exists to protect and work around the addiction. Or there are no rules and children are left to their own devices to raise themselves. Typical rules in a home with addiction are:

  1. Talking about the addiction is forbidden
  2. Don't talk, don't trust, don't feel
  3. Anger can only be expressed when the addict is using (sample: I'm only comfortable showing my feelings – anger or affection - when I'm drunk, high, etc.)

- **Loss of Self** – when people's lives are dominated by emotion, which is the result of living in a tumultuous home with addiction, they become 'fused' or dominated by automatic emotional responses. This differs from a healthy mindset where the person has balance between emotion and intellect. Decision making and coping with stress is much easier for this type of person. They are also more independent. This is not the case with a codependent person.

- **Violence and neglect** – Both are common in families with addiction. One study done in three major metropolitan areas revealed that 78% of all cases of children put into foster care involved substance abuse by the parents. Homicide is only a step away.

- **Emotional damage** – Children raised in households with addiction have negative feelings deeply imbedded, including anger, hate, guilt, blame, and shame.

Often the person who is chemically dependent becomes detached from the rest of the family, lost in addiction. They give up their role as parent and spouse. While the enabler (usually the spouse) is busy supporting the addict, children may assume different roles in the family.

- The Family Hero –Usually the oldest. Tries to do everything perfectly, struggles to be uber responsible and is the 'protector.'

- The Scapegoat – The second child usually assumes this role. Characteristics are: rebellious, antisocial, and troubled. Labeled 'scapegoat' because parents make him the object of their pent up rage and frustration.

- Lost Child – Middle children or the youngest. They get the least amount of attention, especially in a family engulfed by chemical dependency. Followers, not leaders. Engage in a lot of fantasy. May be loners and aren't disruptive, so they slip between the cracks at school, etc. Later in life they often suffer with anxiety and depression. Not risk takers and fear intimacy. Since they are almost invisible at home, they don't cause problems.

- The Mascot/Clown – Usually the youngest. Parents (including the addict) want to protect him. Although the clown makes jokes and keeps people laughing which eases the ongoing tension in the home, inside they are deeply insecure and anxious. As adults, they tend to self medicate.[1]

Can you see yourself anywhere in this list? How about your own children?

Chemical dependency, just as with codependency, is no respecter of income brackets, gender or zip codes. Everything we will be looking at here takes place in the homes of judges and doctors just as often as it does in households where people work for minimum wage or not at all. Although it may look different, the end results are exactly the same. Although women talk about it more, it affects men just as deeply.

Addiction is progressive and if not treated can be lethal. Home life is in constant turmoil due to arguments, lack of boundaries, financial stress, fatigue of the enabler, abuse and all the negative emotions that follow.

The role of abuse

Abuse occurs in many forms and leaves lasting scars on its victims. It's almost always present in one form or another in the backgrounds of codependent people. Important points to look for when recounting abuse in your own life are:

- Abusers can be parent, siblings, relatives, strangers or peers

---

[1]   *Introduction to Addictive Behaviors,* Thombs, 2006.

- Can be verbal, physical, emotional or sexual
- Many victims don't see themselves as abused
- Victims can't feel genuine happiness
- Victims' feelings are hurt easily
- Trust is impossible for victims of abuse
- Victims isolate often in order to cope
- Victims have low self esteem
- When life is going well, victims of abuse get uncomfortable
- Mental confusion exists: feeling mixed up, numb, out of touch with emotions
- Feelings of being dirty, embarrassed, out of control, secretive, appearing guilty
- Develop compulsive behaviors: over eating, drinking, smoking, etc.
- Victims will seek out abusive relationships
- Violent dreams and flashbacks are common
- Become abusers or
- Take on victim-personality
- Suicide and homicide can occur when past abuse is not resolved[2]

Remember, abuse can be created by what is not done: the withholding of affection. It can be the lack of interaction and lack of rules, consequences or overall involvement with the child. It can be accomplished very well by simply ignoring or not talking as a way of manipulating. When this is done without explanation it makes children crazy with guilt and fear because they don't know what they did to deserve it or when it will happen again. Non-parenting (neglect for example) is a very lethal form of abuse.

---

[2]   *Healing the Wounds of Abuse*, Liederman, Resai, 1991

Sometimes it takes a little digging to realize you were subjected to this type of abuse because you may feel like it's all in your head.

The role of shame

There are many character flaws that emerge from being raised by and becoming a codependent. A primary one is shame.

Shame is a powerful word. In what is one of the best books written on the effects of a dysfunctional family, John Bradshaw wrote in *Bradshaw On: The Family*: "Shame is a *being* wound (italics mine) and differs greatly from the feelings of guilt. Guilt says I've *done* something wrong. Shame says there *is* something wrong with me. Guilt says I've *made* a mistake. Shame says I *am* a mistake. Guilt says what I *did* was not good; shame says I *am* no good. The difference makes a profound difference." He goes on to explain that as a result of shame, a 'false self' emerges in order to survive. "The false self forms a defensive mask which distracts from the pain and the inner loneliness of the true self." The **'false self'** is a core issue and something I will refer to throughout this book. Shame is such a fundamental part of abuse that it alone can take a lifetime to overcome.

Not realizing or worse, knowing but not being able or willing to break free of this false self is a sad way to live. Nothing is authentic because long ago we lost ourselves in order to survive. In our place was created a pretend person who became whatever it needed to be, depending on whom it was trying to please. In my experience, this was the quintessential characteristic of codependency and it was borne out of the belief that my true self was too shameful and unacceptable.

> **Vital Sign**
> **A pervasive sense of shame is a common outcome of a**
> **toxic relationship or childhood.**

Based on Bradshaw's powerful book, some of the character traits that an adult from a dysfunctional family might have to deal with are:

- Abandonment issues
- Loneliness
- Thought disorders
- Shame
- Numbed out
- Highly controlling
- Perfectionism
- Intimacy issues
- Secretive
- Poor communication style
- Lack of coping skills
- Compulsive/addictive
- Spiritually bankrupt

This is partial list; his book goes into excellent detail. As you can see, every aspect of your life is affected when shame is inflicted. Each thought, action, response, feeling – everything about who you are has somehow been perverted from how you were meant to be into something whose sole purpose is help you survive the pain of your very existence.

The role of trauma

Peter A. Levine, PhD. is a respected leader in the field of

healing emotional trauma in the body. A more thorough explanation of his research and program is found in the Guide. In his book, *Healing Trauma*, he points out that while all trauma is stressful, not all stress is traumatic. This is important because most of us who ended up saddled with codependency share the root of trauma in our background in one form or another.

Even though his book was *not* about codependency, of the six "Obvious Causes of Trauma" in his book, four of them are directly similar to common events in a codependent household:

1. Severe childhood emotional, physical or sexual abuse
2. Neglect, betrayal or abandonment during childhood
3. Experiencing or witnessing violence
4. Rape

Some of the minor traumas that he included also are found in dysfunctional homes, including being left alone, especially children or babies, and sudden loud noises, common in tumultuous environments.

Acknowledging the importance of the fact that many codependents have trauma in their background is just as important as understanding the role of addiction, abuse and shame. They are common threads that weave into many stories of people who are struggling with codependency and grappling with understanding how this could have happened to them. I am providing the entire outline of trauma symptoms because it will help you not only understand what you are feeling now, but when reading them, you may find yourself remembering images and feelings from times in your past.

The first symptoms of trauma, when the event is about to occur or is happening, according to Levine include:

- Denial
- Dissociation
- Feelings of helplessness, immobility and freezing
- Hyper-arousal (increase in heart rate, sweating, difficulty breathing, cold sweats, and muscular tension)
- Constriction – the body is tense and prepared to take defensive action. This is when one may feel numb or shut down

  Other early symptoms that begin to show up shortly after or during trauma can include:
- Hyper-vigilance; on guard at all times
- Intrusive imagery or flashbacks
- Extreme sensitivity to light and sound
- Hyperactivity
- Exaggerated emotional and startle responses
- Nightmares and night terrors
- Abrupt mood swings
- Shame and lack of self-worth
- Reduced ability to deal with stress (easily and frequently stressed out)
- Difficulty sleeping.

Years later, according to Levine, other symptoms can show up such as:
- Panic attacks, anxiety, and phobias
- Mental 'blankness' or spaced-out feelings
- Avoidance behavior
- Attraction to dangerous situations
- Addictive behaviors (overeating, drinking, smoking, etc.)
- Exaggerated or diminished sexual activity
- Amnesia and forgetfulness

- Inability to love, nurture or bond with other people
- Fear of dying or having a shortened life
- Self-mutilation
- Loss of sustaining beliefs (spiritual, religious, interpersonal)

Finally, he lists the symptoms that take longer to develop. He points out that usually, some of the earlier symptoms show up first. The last group includes:
- Excessive shyness
- Diminished emotional responses
- Inability to make commitments
- Chronic fatigue or very low physical energy
- Immune system problems and certain endocrine problems such as thyroid
- Malfunction and environmental sensitivities
- Psychosomatic illnesses, i.e. headaches, migraines, neck/ back pains
- Chronic pain
- Fibromyalgia
- Asthma
- Skin disorders
- Digestive problems (spastic colon)
- Severe menstrual syndrome
- Depression and feelings of impending doom
- Feelings of detachment, alienation and isolation ('living dead' feelings)
- Reduced ability to formulate plans

Dr. Levine writes that symptoms of trauma can be ever-present, come and go and be triggered by stress or they can remain hidden for decades and suddenly surface. In addition, they often grow more complex over time and become less and less connected with the original trauma experience.

Can you see why it's vital to be aware of your body, thoughts and actions? You may be experiencing physical issues which are a direct result of a traumatic event that happened so long ago you don't even remember it. Yet, that event or multiple events not only formed your character, it may be creating serious health issues for you today. We will go into detail about this important aspect of healing in the Guide.

Finally, he talks about the 'compulsion to repeat' which as we have already discussed is a hallmark attribute of a codependent. He writes, *"We are inextricably drawn into situations that replicate the original trauma in both obvious and less obvious ways....re-enactments may be played out in intimate relationships, work situations....they may also appear in the form of bodily symptoms or psychosomatic diseases."*

Notice that although Dr. Levine isn't talking about codependency, the tendencies are the same.

Tying all four together- how they create codependency

The important fact that emerges after looking at addiction, abuse, shame and trauma is this: *many of the same powerful characteristics and outcomes which are found in each one also fall right into the list of traits describing codependency.* They are strikingly intertwined. Look at each list of symptoms again. The similarity is undeniable. If you are codependent, you will see yourself over and over again on the previous pages. This means your fight for emotional freedom won't be over until codependency is recognized, understood and overcome.

Based on the previous information, combined with

everything else spelled out up to this point, it becomes clear why it is so important to learn what made you codependent, how it is influencing your life on every level and how to heal. How they are interconnected is important when putting the puzzle together. The finished image is, of course, the face of codependency; the hardest of all to understand.

There is one more important aspect of all of this to be considered:

Codependency is contagious

One of the most egregious effects of being codependent is that we set up role models for our children which teach them to be exactly like us, thereby perpetuating the cycle. How you respond to stress, form relationships and the way you handle yourself everyday is not lost on them.

Kids pick up on everything. They are watching as you jump from one relationship to another, with all the drama and chaos. Or at the other extreme, they stand on the sidelines, anxiously observing as you remain in an unhealthy marriage or partnership. They worry as they see you agonizing over endless problems and stress. They feel helpless and responsible when they see how worn out and emotionally fragile you are. Even if they don't or can't verbalize it, they are soaking up your anxiety, guilt, worry, shame; all of it is becoming part of their make-up, too. While you are caught up in your own problems, they are becoming either too mature for their age out of a perceived necessity, or at the opposite extreme, too immature for their age because they are scared and overwhelmed. The tendency for over-attachment out of fear is ever present.

The pattern of dysfunction is set to repeat itself as they form their own relationships, learn to solve their own problems the same way you do and develop their own negative self-image. They are doomed to the same unhappy fate you've experienced so far if you don't make the decision to do whatever it takes to change. This includes the propensity for hooking up with dangerous, dysfunctional or mentally unstable people as adults and eventually abusing or neglecting their own children as they spin out of emotional control. If you haven't had the strength or courage make the choice to stop this cycle up until this moment, I implore you to do it for your children.

Part of the codependent syndrome is that we live in denial. You probably have convinced yourself that your kids are fine. They are not. They may be acting 'fine' because they think if they did one little thing to upset you, it might cause you to have a nervous breakdown. On the other hand, you could be so lost in your own drama, so depressed or caught up in someone else's struggle with addiction - maybe even your own- that you aren't doing your job as a parent and aren't tuned in to your children's needs at all. This is a terrible price for a child to pay for your problems. Isn't this similar to what you grew up with? Do you really want to pass it on to your kids?

Understanding what codependency is, how it is the outcome of powerful influences such as addiction, abuse, trauma and shame; and finally the fact that you will pass it on to your children if you don't reverse course, has hopefully made you hungry for some help.

You are making a brave, difficult but not impossible choice to recover. Not just from codependency, but from wrong thinking, past hurts and the endless craziness you emerged from and are still coping with. You may be the first in your entire family to recognize this generational problem, so don't expect much support from those around you who are all players in your story. Anyone who has walked down this path discovers quickly that this will be a journey you make alone.

What does a healthy family look like?

For the sake of comparison, answer "yes" or "no" to these questions.

1. Did you feel appropriately loved as a child?__
2. Did you feel acknowledged and heard?__
3. Were you encouraged to pursue your interests?__
4. Did you feel safe expressing yourself without fearing for consequences?__
5. Was there an absence of daily emotional stress?___
6. Were you loved for who you were – not your accomplishments?__
7. Were personal boundaries respected?__
8. Was there playfulness and laughter?__
9. Did you feel secure?__
10. Was okay to disagree without feeling rejected?__

These questions paint a broad picture of a stable, nurturing environment. In families like this the parent loves, encourages, teaches and protects the child. The child is free to enjoy being who he is instead of worrying about whether the parents are going to criticize, reject, ridicule or punish him. The parental role is assumed by the adults. The child isn't made to feel responsible for the adult's happiness or wellbeing. Was this what you came from? Neither did I.

Creation of a codependent

I knew I would have to share my history to write this book,

but every time I sat down to begin, it only took a few pages for me to realize I hadn't come to the bottom of my own story. The more layers of the onion I peeled back, the bigger and more overwhelming the onion got. It didn't seem right to write a book about something I had not completely finished experiencing.

Then I got a revelation: there is no end. There's just another layer. Time was going by. While I still have work to do, I've come a long, long way and there was much I wanted to share. Waiting for the perfect time was a ridiculous goal. In order to be taken seriously, it is important that the reader know I had been there and had managed to overcome the deep-seated fear that I really was crazy. But I will always have to be on my guard for those old codependent tendencies that want to creep into my thinking on occasion. The only difference is now I am mindful of how I think, behave and function in the world. This difference took me from dysfunctional to balanced. It doesn't mean I don't relapse into destructive thinking from time to time. I'm not without flaws. That's the thinking of a true codependent: "I must be perfect or I am nothing!" Just being able to get past this lie was a huge step for me.

While putting into words what I remembered, I began to fear that the truth wasn't even noteworthy. This was terrifying. What if it was all in my head? After all, I hadn't been tortured, neglected or anything headline worthy. But then many people who struggle with codependency came from what could be viewed as normal backgrounds. However, there is often a common denominator which can't be seen until they are looked at more deeply.

For instance, what I had experienced was especially frightening exactly because it was not the stuff that makes the news. For the most part it was inconspicuous. *Emotional abuse-which is often done in the form of withholding love and affection - is an invisible but incredibly powerful weapon.* All of it culminated in forming me into one thoroughly codependent person.

What happened to me was a case of mal-nurturing. I was given constant messages whether in words, actions or manipulation which said I was bad, stupid, shameful; a bother. Although these concepts had devastating effects on me, they sound so minor, almost petty in comparison to the types of abuse which can be seen.

Yet when I look hard to see how insidious and damaging those messages really were, it's obvious the end result was just as damaging, if not more than outward, physical, aggression. Unfortunately, as I will get into later, there was some of that as well. Realizing this made it imperative for me to remember (and I have a terrible time with this) what *wasn't* there.

Nurturing *wasn't* there. Nothing I did seemed to please my mother, who was in a perpetual state of angst. I know now my mother saw me as an extension of herself. Since she was insecure and had been raised in a shame-based environment, nothing about me was ever quite perfect enough. I was simply another thing for her to feel ashamed about. Although I was always provided for – we always had three square meals a day and clean clothes; I never had the sense she or my father enjoyed having me around. Quite the opposite.

What *wasn't* there was a father to protect me and love me in a manner I could depend on. I was a nervous wreck because one day my dad was kissing me goodnight on the cheek and calling me 'Queen', the next he was spewing out hateful words like "You're nothing, you're no good, and you're stupid." In short, I felt crazy at an early age because I never knew from moment to moment, day to day what to expect. Minimum displays of affection were replaced with explosive bursts of rage when the drinking started.

The sound of the phone ringing made me jump out of my

skin and my stomach would clench because it meant my dad was ready to be picked up - and he was drunk. What happened when he stumbled through the front door was anybody's guess, but it was never good. What *wasn't* there was stability.

The constant nagging and pressure my mother put on us (meaning my sibling and me, but I only have the right to tell my own story) nearly drove me to madness early in life. Nothing was ever right or good enough. What *wasn't* there was empowerment at any level.

From an early memory of her pulling on my braids in a frustrated, spiteful way as she put them together, to years later when she literally threw me out of her house because my own little daughter made too much of a mess; and all the years in between lead to me the undeniable conclusion I was too much for her. I just didn't know why. The constant message I got was something was wrong with me. Nothing I ever did could extract the love I so desperately craved. It was only fitting she passed the same sense of disappointment on to her grandchildren, a decision which has left scars on my oldest daughter as well as my niece's to this day. She managed to poison a whole new generation with her hateful behavior.

As I mentioned earlier, there were plenty of physical brawls, too. It wasn't the usual child getting beaten by the parent, but rather the child and adult going at it in ludicrous acts of rage. Surely, nothing could be more dysfunctional than an environment where this was permitted right under the nose of one's mother. I was a skinny fifteen year old girl when it was acceptable for me to be the one between my mother and father. It added to the craziness and was just one more big secret to add to our family's private collection of shame. What *wasn't* there, over all, was a calm, loving home in which to grow up normally.

All this happened so long ago but the effects still rock me from time to time. I carry guilt that I do not feel especially affectionate toward my mother, who is now an eighty-six year old fragile woman with alcohol-induced dementia. Spending time with her leaves me exhausted because I do it out of obligation, not because I enjoy it. Any opportunity to talk things out has been washed away by too many bottles of cheap wine. Her mind is like a honeycomb – full of holes. No thought stays long enough to really be effectively considered. It's too late.

I feel remorse I never really got to know my father who died of emphysema at 72. We didn't talk about anything, except when we were fighting. Then there was lots of screaming and cursing.

I'm told he adored me as a baby. I wish I could remember that love, but I don't. He was a career enlisted Army soldier. He was either physically gone, or home and mentally checked out. When he was sober, he was like a church mouse, trying to stay out of mom's way; very quiet. My mother emasculated him by taking charge early in their relationship. Nothing he did was ever right, either. He drank to escape. Then he had beer muscle and liked to throw it around. The next day, he was just a quiet little hung over mealy-mouthed man who would try to block out my mother's endless nagging and pleadings by mumbling things in agreement just to shut her up. Eventually he'd grab his hat and walk out the door. Then we would wait for the phone to ring and the whole miserable cycle would start all over again. I clung to those precious mid-week days when he was just a sort-of-normal father who went to work and came home with little gifts, like colored pencils he stole from the military base where he worked - another little character flaw.

From time to time, however, he'd go on a 'bender' where he would miss work and drink for days on end which really cranked up the stress level in our house. We were on perpetual alert during those awful stretches of time. Life was unpredictable and scary.

In the midst of all this, we would methodically cling to things which represented normal. My brother and I had to adhere to an endless list of rules. Things were rigid; tense. Spontaneity was unheard of. We cleaned house on Saturday which meant I would do a chore and mother would be right behind me doing it over, grumbling and banging things around as she griped about how I couldn't do anything right. We went to church on Sunday morning and in the evening mother did ironing in the basement while humming along to her favorite German music. When she was left alone, she at last had some peace, which meant I could relax. My dad remained slouched in his chair, staring at something on television none of us enjoyed, going through bottle after bottle of beer, so we left him alone. I hid in my room. We had dinner at five while watching the news every weekday. Being forced to eat while trying not to watch the endless pictures of dead soldiers in Vietnam was still better than having to talk to each other. On weekends, we had to work around my dad's dramatic comings and goings. In other words, we functioned as well as we could. Most of the time I felt anxious and numb. I did what I was told. Talking back was not an option. Meanwhile the rage was mounting inside me. The world around us had no idea of the craziness that was going on inside our house.

When I allow myself to see my early years from this vantage point, it's easy to see how confusing and utterly dysfunctional my upbringing was. It left me leaving feeling pessimistic, scared, lonely, insecure, resentful, anxious, unlovable, lost, confused and full of anger. By the time I was sixteen, I was contemplating murder.

I shot out of that petri dish of emotional squalor we called home as soon as I was old enough to get my own place. Naturally, it didn't take long for things to unravel even more from there. Dysfunction was all I had ever known, so of course I continued to spin more of it completely unaware of how I was sabotaging myself.

Generational codependency – looking deeper into the family dynamic

Clearly there were problems in our family. Yes, my father was an alcoholic. He was also a frightened, lost, insecure little man with lots of secrets. He was an underachiever with no real self confidence, just a foul mouth when he drank. His story is a mystery to me even today. Everything about him seemed to be off limits. When a question about his past ever surfaced, it was quickly dismissed by my mother with a wave of the hand and a sideways glance. "I don't know about that," was the usual response. Once again, an intense sense of shame hung in the air. We were left in the dark to make up our own stories. No extended family ever contacted or visited us, which only added to my sense of loneliness and lack of belonging. The exception was his mother who religiously sent both my brother and me cards for birthdays and Christmas with $5 in them when we were young. I don't recall ever speaking to her. There were no pictures of his family in the house. It was all a big mystery and off limits.

He needed my mother to not only cover for him, but to take his place as the father figure and head of the household. My father was the *dependent* in their relationship. He was dependent on the liquor and in the fashion of these types of relationships; he was dependent on my mother to make sure he could continue in his addiction.

My mother was the *enabler*. She did everything she could to contain his problem but also helped him stay addicted to keep the peace. She picked him up whenever he called. She bought him booze and cigarettes so he wouldn't leave the house and embarrass us even more as he staggered down the sidewalks of our little town. She served him dinner in his chair while we huddled over our plates in my upstairs bedroom which doubled as our sanctuary when he was drunk. Most of all, she kept secrets. She never told anyone. She pretended things were fine. She made excuses. She drove herself crazy taking care of the house, the bills, us kids and even took on a full time job on an assembly line when I was in high school. She was exhausted most of the time. I remember her occasionally having terrible back pain that landed her in bed for days. Many years later she admitted she used to wish she could go to the hospital for a few days just to rest.

The most damaging aspect of her unintended role as protector of her husband's addiction was that in the process, she conceded her role as protector of her children. Otherwise, how could she just stand there as my father and I engaged in physical fights?

My mother was critical, controlling, over-bearing, moody and impatient. I tried to stay out of her way most of the time. In my little girl eyes, she was scary and I dreaded being in her presence. I didn't know her as the sad, bitter, insecure and worn out woman she also was. All I saw was a mother who –try as I did – would not give me one thing I needed most: acceptance. How could I know she was also codependent? The word hadn't even come into our lexicon yet.

When my father was terminally ill, she did her best to take care of him while still holding down a full time job. Even though he could barely draw a breath anymore due to a lifetime of smoking, she still bought him cigarettes so he wouldn't try to walk down to the store. I'm sure in her enabler-minded way she thought she was doing the right thing.

I was confident if I got sick, she would take good care of me, because that was her great skill: caretaking. The rest of the time I was just a source of aggravation. My mother was codependent in the truest sense. Her life revolved around making sure everything in our home was under control because her world was so maddeningly out of control due to my father's addiction. She was just as much a prisoner to his drinking as he was.

But to be fair, she was already programmed to be the one in control due to her traumatic life as a young woman in war-torn Germany. Her story could easily be its own book. The short version of her story is she was raised in a culture where children were not coddled. They were instead expected to start chipping in on the household duties at a very young age. In addition, the terror and loss of living through a world war unfolding in the streets of her town wore on her in more ways than I'm sure I'll ever know.

My mother is now eighty-six and still lives alone in her house with a cat. Often I watch as she yells at the poor thing for doing cat-like things. "Shame on you!" she hisses, shaking her crooked finger at the innocent creature who, thankfully doesn't care. My heart beats faster every time I see her do that. It causes old feelings to bubble up and I can only assume I was shamed like that from an early age, I'm guessing for doing child-like things. Shame! Shame! It is no surprise to me that in every picture of me as a small child, I have a distant, vacant look in my eyes. The shame factor had taken root early. My light – the free spirit within an innocent child - was stifled very early in life. In its place settled in the heaviness of fear and shame.

One guaranteed outcome of being codependent was that I continually sought out the same type of dysfunctional relationships, exactly as Dr. Levine pointed out.

Doomed to repeat my behavior because I didn't know better and had zero confidence, I went from one unhealthy relationship, affair, friendship, and association to the next, all the while wondering why the same disastrous results kept occurring.

> **Vital Sign**
>
> The first step to being whole again is to remember
>
> what it is that you're trying to overcome.
>
> Remembering the past is vital.
>
> Staying lost in it will cost you everything.

Remembering is a tool

I have years of nothingness in my past; entire years I do not remember. The times I do recall are scarred with scenarios that just don't fit into typical childhood memories.

For instance, as I mentioned earlier, I seriously contemplated murder when I was sixteen. Instead of worrying about what to wear to prom (I didn't get asked anyway), I sat in my bedroom calculating how many years I'd spend in prison if I killed my father and how old I'd be when I got out. After doing the numbers, I decided it would be worth it. I have a memory of holding a large knife and trying to lunge at my dad while my mother was screaming and holding me back. Not a "Leave it to Beaver" moment.

Now I realize my situation, though bizarre, is not uncommon, but back then, I felt completely and utterly isolated, not to mention crazy. So much of what happened in those years is gone from my memory, even though I remember vowing to myself often, "I am never going to forget this because I want to remember why I am so angry!" But I didn't write those events down and they eventually faded from memory.

I couldn't have a sleep over like other girls for fear my dad might embarrass me in some mortifying way. Holidays were lonely and heavy. With no extended family anywhere and the unspoken rule that outsiders weren't welcome, we ate, did the dishes and got as far away from each other as possible. I usually headed up to my room and got lost in the stories I would write, which is where my writing began. All things work for good.

I also mentioned briefly in the beginning that my mother dragged us to a Lutheran church every Sunday. My father, a fallen Catholic, was noticeably relieved to see us go. At least he could be hung over in peace for a couple of hours. Going to church was just another stressful exercise in trying to be normal and a leftover ritual from mother's upbringing. It was all about getting there early to get a good parking spot. This meant anxiously rushing around in a panic while my mother scowled and barked out commands to hurry up. Upon arrival to church, we always sat near the back so, God forbid, no one should see us. We had to hurry up and be one of the first ones out too, in order to beat the traffic. That was our stressful roundtrip routine. Never in all those nerve-wracked Sundays do I recall our family ever once talking about what we heard at church. It was just another part of the effort to maintain control and a sense of normalcy. Redemption wasn't part of the equation.

Earlier I mentioned the fact that my father and I would go at it physically on occasion. I've mercifully forgotten most of them, but one sticks in my memory. He had made a threat to my mother. An uncontrollable rage engulfed me and without thinking I lunged at him as he came to the second story stairs where we were standing. My arms were clenched around his neck as we stumbled down two flights. I was screaming, kicking him, clawing at his face and he was cussing at me. It was almost comical in a sick way. We ended up in the basement. When I finally disengaged, crying and hyperventilating, he yelled at me, "If you ever jump me again, I'll kill you!" He had to miss work for a couple days due to the scratches on his face. I was about fifteen and filled with anger after years of his verbal and emotional abuse not just toward me, but to my mother as well. I felt a momentary sense of victory, and even cracked a sheepish smile because my dad had let loose a string of profanities which had only added to the appalling wrongness of what had just happened. But more importantly, I felt abandoned. Why did I have to do this? Why didn't someone, meaning my own mother, help me? A feeling I couldn't even put into words, but now I realize was shame permeated my being. Who does this type of thing? It was sick and perverted. That moment became the center stone of my self-image: bad, wrong, *shameful* and utterly alone. That shame combined with an ever festering rage at both my father and mother made it impossible for me to function like a normal teenager. I was already deeply affected by my parent's addiction and codependency. I just didn't know it yet.

As far back as elementary school I suffered from anxiety, depression and was always fearful. I was withdrawn, insecure and didn't have good boundaries because I was so hungry for acceptance. But no one talked about such things back then. I lived in the shadows just to avoid more drama.

One of the tragedies of my childhood trauma is I got derailed off my path before I had a chance to get started. Instead of enjoying school, friends or delighting in dreams that seem so possible for everyone else, as a traumatized child I was forced to deal with issues that were completely not age appropriate, as a result, I lost my precious childhood.

I developed characteristics of someone with Post Traumatic Stress: I couldn't concentrate, was overly sensitive, was easily frightened and was sick constantly. Only recently have I come to understand that my body was crying out in retaliation to what was happening.

By the time I got to high school, I worried constantly about what was going to happen at home each day. I felt invisible when I watched those other kids having so much fun, teasing and joking with each other. I might as well have been an alien watching from another planet. Although I wasn't bad looking, I was terribly self-conscious, lonely and had a pervasive sense of impending doom hanging over me.

Of course anger was always bubbling within me, but I was not allowed to express it. Feeling depleted, in a fog and sad became a way of life for me early on.

Later in my one-year, half-hearted attempt at college, I met a young man in an English class which resulted in a whole new level of physical, emotional and verbal abuse. Before I knew what was happening, BAM! I was one ring of fire closer to hell on earth.

These are some pieces of my early years I had to look at in order to overcome my problems. But the reasons for my striving to be 'normal' as an adult weren't just for my sake. I now had two lovely daughters who I was setting a less than ideal example for. I had the inner drive to make my own life better, but I also had a responsibility to see to it that what happened to me was not repeated. I'm thankful I was aware of that in spite of my mess.

I was in my late twenties when I took the first step of discovering and accepting that I was codependent, then another and kept going for thirty years. I had to or I would have either still been in some sick relationship or committed suicide long ago.

Here is the truth that changed my life:

When I understood I no longer needed to play by the dysfunctional, harsh rules I accepted as a child, I began the process of dismantling my **false self.**

When I quit the never-ending battle of living to meet everyone else's needs while ignoring my own, I no longer felt crazy. In other words, when I realized I was codependent, I took the first step to a better life. Freedom is on the other side of codependency. Keep walking.

Moving past surviving into overcoming

For years the term I heard over and over again was 'survivor' whenever I let someone have a peak at my shameful past.

Even though there was some solace in knowing I had survived something, it conjured up an image of a half dead, ravaged soul hanging on to a piece of driftwood in murky waters, exhausted and disoriented after a flood. I had survived. Now what. I didn't change the weather or flee the oncoming disaster. I was caught up in something completely out of my control which left me clinging to life, drained but at least with a pulse. I had survived to fight my demons another day.

Even as an adult, when I finally disengaged from an abusive relationship and began carving out a new life in another state, my thinking was just as messed up as ever. I was highly controlling, moody, had poor boundaries and was terribly insecure. I didn't trust anyone and was in denial about just how screwed up I was because I was spending all my time trying to either fix those around me, or was lost in a stew of anger at my past. In addition, I had a list of physical ailments (anemia, fatigue, frequent sickness, severe menstrual cycles – again, just as described by Dr. Levine earlier) I was the embodiment of codependency. All this was just under the surface while I pretended to be whatever was required in order to be accepted by the people I was with hour to hour. Keeping rejection at bay and somehow fitting in was my secret goal in life and it was killing me. This hardly seemed like any sort of victory, though in the rawest sense it was a beginning.

It was a combination of desperation and divine intervention that got me away from my beginnings so I could at least survive. The hard work of undoing the effects of those first twenty two years and becoming an overcomer was yet to be done. It turned into a lifetime mission and I don't think it will ever really be finished. As long as I remain self-aware, I will always be watching out for those old behaviors to return out of habit and I will have to make the conscious decision not to let them continue.

Codependency – just one card in the deck of disorders

As a child and young adult, there was no way I could have known that what I was coping with day to day was gradually turning me into an exact replica of my mother's anxious, compulsive, controlling nature combined with my father's erratic, unstable tendencies. I was busy trying to get through one day at a time. In the process, I was picking up negative traits that eventually overshadowed and replaced any healthy characteristics trying to emerge.

Being well-grounded, having strong self esteem and most important, feeling safe, normal and deserving of a place in this life eluded me. I do not recall having one single day of inner peace for decades. Instead, I was haunted by guilt and an unexplainable emptiness which I later came to understand was depression.

For years, I had no idea what I felt, who I was, or if what I was thinking was real or crazy. My false self had taken over and my authentic self had gone dormant. In short, I had disappeared. I simply took on the personality of those around me to fit in, often with negative results. In other words, my false self ran the show because my authentic self was cowering in a corner of my mind, too scared to talk.

Unsafe, non-nurturing environments where children are either physically and/or emotionally traumatized which as I explained earlier, includes the lack of interaction and can be the start of many lifelong problems. These include the development of bi-polar disorder, borderline personality, post-traumatic stress, anxiety, narcissism, obsessive-compulsive disorder and of course, codependency. Many times they work in tandem, meaning you might have to unravel and overcome the effects any combination of disorders along with codependency. The same can be said of anyone raised in a chaotic, unloving, cruel or in any way dysfunctional home.

Vital Sign

You can be codependent and have other disorders as well. In fact, it's quite likely. It's important to find a good therapist and really get to understand who you are. This is one job you simply shouldn't have to do by yourself.

If you have sought out help and have been given a couple of labels to contend with, odds are you can overcome them. Not by blinking your eyes and making it so, as was the Charlie Sheen method (recalling his humiliating meltdown in the media's eye several years ago), but by a conscious decision to do what it takes to get yourself whole again. *Remember, you didn't come into this world broken. You were made that way somewhere along the line.*

I was one of those who got dealt several of those cards. I don't believe my parents set out to do damage to me. But because they were hurting so badly themselves, they unintentionally managed to saddle me with a myriad of problems I eventually had to identify and work out. All of it stemmed from codependency at work in their lives, they just didn't know it.

My story demonstrates that codependency isn't just confined to extreme cases of abuse. In addition, it serves as a reminder that in most cases, those who raised us were also damaged from the burdens of their own past. It's important to understand, however, that even though my background did revolve around chemical dependency, this is not the only scenario in which codependency can emerge in a person's character.

What lies behind

"If you bring forth that which is within you,
Then that which is within you
Will be your salvation.
If you do not bring forth that which is within you,
Then that which is within you
Will destroy you."
– The Gnostic Gospels[3]

It was necessary for me to share a little bit of my history with you. But the important point to remember is *you* are the reason for this book, not me. You are probably tired of looking back, but to fully understand your story and how it brought you here, we need to start and the beginning. This means recalling what and why you are on the journey to overcome in the first place, just as I had to.

It wasn't easy to put my humiliating childhood on paper for all to see, but it was an important first step in my own healing years ago. It's time for you to do the same.

Starting here, I ask that you begin the job of facing whatever has a choke-hold on your soul so you can be an overcomer as well. It's going to require some effort to get there.

If you haven't done this kind of work before, it may be hard to put the pieces together. Or maybe it'll be crystal clear. If you have done exercises like these in the past, do them again here. You'll need

---

[3]   *from 'Healing Trauma,' Peter Levine, 2008*

to keep your written responses in one place to refer to again when we get to the Guide. Remembering is the key. This presents a problem for those who have successfully blocked some memories in order to endure the pain, as was my case. Do the best you can.

A word of caution: because what happened to you may be buried in the distant past, there is a tendency to minimize the effect it had on you. This is normal but just another lie. I fought those feelings for many years. They all resurfaced while writing this book. Time does have a way of erasing from our minds how awful the things we went through really were. Decades later I found myself wondering, 'Why do I still let that bother me? It wasn't so bad.' *This is minimizing which is a form of denial.* If you try to justify your thoughts this way, these truths will help:

1) Your memory does fade so you may in fact not even remember how scared, hurt, abandoned, enraged or traumatized you actually felt.

2) Minimizing our experiences is a coping mechanism.

3) As I explained at the beginning, some devastating abuses cannot be seen, only sensed. Those can leave the biggest impressions on the psyche of a child, especially if the lack of interaction was involved. Remember what *wasn't* there.

4) Finally, ask yourself this: if it really wasn't all that bad, then why have you spent your life trying to get past the effects it had on you? Think of it this way: just because the horrific car wreck you were just in gets smaller and smaller in the rear view mirror of the ambulance that's taking you away from the scene of the carnage, doesn't mean it didn't happen.

Keep these factors in mind as you do the work coming up.

What did you have to deal with?

Let's start with the basic outline of your home life. Describe your family of origin's dynamic. How was your home life? Do you remember what your relationship with your parents or those who raised you was like? Did you feel safe, terrified, belittled, over indulged, anxious, angry or lonely? If your memories are happy and seemingly well-adjusted note that, too. Be as detailed as possible. Remember, minimizing your experiences was a way of coping. Do not let yourself do that here. This may seem too painful or may conjure up unbearable anger or other destructive emotions. Remember, none of it can hurt you anymore. No one ever died from a feeling. Go slowly. If you need to stop and take a walk or do something else for a while, that's okay. Use more paper if necessary. We are going at your speed. When you're ready, the page is waiting.

_____

_____

_____

_____

_____

Self image

As a child, I had the definite feeling I was different; less than others in an indefinable way. I can't say I was aware of a 'self image' – no one talked in those terms back then. All I knew growing up was I felt invisible. Perhaps a poignant moment that clarifies this is one small memory I have. I was walking on the cracked sidewalk in front of our house on a warm day. I know I had braids and was wearing a dress because I remember looking at my knees. I recall saying out loud, or at least hearing myself thinking, "Maybe if I had a limp, someone would notice me." Pitiful, pitiful.

This tiny flash of a memory summed up my whole belief about myself as a little girl. I didn't matter unless I was really sick. My mother was great in a crisis – another indicator of being codependent. Otherwise, I was just an annoyance; in the way, or so it felt to me, especially when my parents were arguing or acting out.

Let this example help you recall and write down the general image you had of yourself during your early life. What were some beliefs you had? Did you even have a self view, or were you too numb? What were the messages your parents gave you? Were you told you were good, bad, smart, stupid, loved, hated, in the way, an embarrassment or did they make you feel special? Were you acknowledged for what you accomplished rather than for who you were? Were you ignored? Did you get put in the position too early of having to be the parent? It could be you have a combination of positives and negatives. As was the case with my father, the sense of feeling safe one day and crazy scared the next was because the messages were so mixed. These are big questions but will help you as you read on, so take your time. Let yourself go back and feel those childhood emotions. Be specific.

_____

_____

_____

_____

_____

_____

Many survivors/overcomers of addiction, abuse, trauma or shame-based upbringings have sought out help, such as therapy, support groups, etc. Some go for a while; others do it their whole lives. I started out by seeing a social worker when I was twenty and I will always believe she saved me. For the first time in my young life, someone listened, accepted and assured me that among other things my depression would not last forever. She gave me hope when I was at the end of my rope and couldn't see a way out. I saw many counselors after that, read hundreds of books, went to seminars, support groups, church, prayed, sought out good role models, tried different medications for depression and anxiety. I devoted my life to getting better.

What about you? List what types of help you've undertaken. If you have not had any such help, just note that and continue on.

_____

_____

_____

_____

_____

_____

_____

If you have sought help, have you made progress or are you stuck? Write down how you view yourself now as opposed to how you saw yourself before you began the hard work of breaking free of your past. If you are just beginning your work, start by writing down what it is in particular you believe you need to work on first and what steps you know deep inside you need to take. Be realistic. I had to get my anxiety and depression under control first before I could even focus on learning about what made me tick and how to change. What is going on right now?

_____

_____

_____

_____

_____

What events or triggers would result in negative action against you? It could be something you did that you were yelled at or punished for. You might have been an innocent bystander when some behaved badly, like a drunken father on a tirade. Were you the victim of sexual, physical, emotional or verbal assault? Were you simply ignored, left to wonder why? If you experienced trauma, did you feel angry, different, frightened, nervous, anxious, like a fraud, dirty, depressed, and empty; or did you disappear, watching from above as you split away to not feel the pain of the experience?

_____

_____

_____

Recall my story about how my heart raced and my stomach clenched when our phone rang. Now remember your own feelings and put down the descriptive words. Was it the sounds of your father's footsteps approaching your door? Do it quickly, don't ponder it. Taking too much time will encourage you to get lost in those moments again and that isn't going to help you. Be detached in your recollections, if possible.

_____

_____

_____

_____

_____

Were you sexually or physically abused? Describe it to the best of your ability.

_____

_____

_____

_____

_____

How did you cope? Did you mentally split off and watch from somewhere else in the room? Did you fight? Were you compliant due to fear or emotional retaliation? Who did it? Did you tell anyone or did you keep secrets? Let yourself remember to the extent you can.

_____

_____

_____

_____

_____

_____

What were you feeling/thinking during these events? What sensations or particular images stick in your memory? What was the message you got? How did it impact your life later?

_____

_____

_____

_____

_____

What was a typical form of emotional, verbal or mental abuse you encountered? Remember, withholding love, displays of affection or ignoring also leave the same scars.

_____

_____

_____

_____

_____

How did you get past the pain, fear, anger or whatever negative emotions you experienced in those times? Describe any hobbies, outlets, actions, places you would go, things you would do that took your mind off your life. Include any negative methods of coping. Did you do self-harm, indulge in substance abuse, pick fights, break or otherwise damage things, run away, stay out of the house as long as possible, or simply shutdown?

_____

_____

_____

_____

_____

_____

What childhood sicknesses did you have, other than the usual? Were you sick often? Were you properly tended to? What are your memories in this area?

_____

_____

_____

_____

_____

As an adult, did you or do you suffer from any physical problems? Explain.

_____

_____

_____

_____

_____

_____

If you believe you have become codependent as a result of an adult relationship you were or are currently in, describe what that relationship looks like. Who is the strong one; the weak one? Do you find yourself trying to fix, control or please the other person to the extent it is exhausting you? Describe how you see yourself (overly responsible, compulsive, jealous, insecure, depressed, anxious, scared...anything that comes to mind.) What is going on in this relationship that is controlling and overwhelming you?

_____

_____

_____

_____

_____

Now briefly describe the other person and how you feel about him/her.

_____

_____

_____

_____

_____

Answer yes or no to the following: Have you been in similar relationships before?

_____

If so, how did they end?

_____

_____

_____

Is addiction of any kind - drugs, alcohol, food, spending, sex - involved in your life or family now? Who is the enabler or caretaker? Describe it.

_____

_____

_____

_____

_____

Vital Sign

Not all dysfunctional behavior is rooted in childhood. Some people enter into unhealthy relationships as adults where they develop unhealthy coping mechanisms to survive.

Life is hard. It's harder when you've got the unresolved burdens of your painful past cooped up in your mind like a crazed demon screeching to be heard, clawing at the walls to be set free.

At this moment you have only your own will to survive keeping that loathsome creature in your head powerless and mute on a moment to moment basis. I don't have to tell you how all-consuming this effort is. It's no surprise you are exhausted all the time even if you have nothing visible to show for your spent energy. The fatigue alone leaves you feeling a little crazy. It does not have to stay this way. You are about to change.

What lies ahead

So far, we've focused on the tough job of looking back at sources of pain that caused, among other things, your descent into codependency.

Here's the good part: you have a bright, normal future ahead of you, if you want it badly enough. The word 'normal' makes me a little uncomfortable because it insinuates someone other than us gets to determine the standard. Let's agree *normal* is another word for *healthy* which is not to be confused with *average*.

Vital Sign

Being average is difficult for the codependent because we get our 'worth' out of being perfect and exhaust ourselves trying. In our unbalanced way of thinking, once we buy into the concept that whatever we are trying to do will never be good enough, we go to the other extreme and choose to become complete failures. Average is impossible and unnatural for this type of mindset.

In my seemingly endless state of feeling crazy, I aspired to be average. Long ago, I would watch with awe and envy at people who seemed normal. I would pray, "God, I just want to have a normal life." To me this meant not getting beaten for something as meaningless as glancing at a man who happened to be in my line of vision which was part of my time with the guy from college. It meant not jumping when the phone rang or when something fell and made a loud sound as a child. It meant not having awful fights behind closed doors while pretending to be okay in the world. **Most of all, it meant I would be able to get that 'parent in my head' to shut-up, once and for all and end the non-stop messages telling me nothing I did was perfect enough, making me feel like a complete, damaged failure.** When I would see couples and families living such 'normal', happy, well-adjusted, average lives, it just seemed like an impossible fantasy which would never be possible for me.

When I look at my life now, while it certainly isn't perfect, I think most people would agree it's pretty normal. This is the miracle of persistence. There were so many times when I wanted to give up. Sometimes I did. Like most people though, I didn't have the luxury of just curling up in a ball for weeks at a time. I had responsibilities and I learned from experience the dark tunnel my mind – depression - would eventually come to an end. Believing it would pass kept me going, but it wasn't easy. It usually became a waiting game between my pain and my will: "It's never going to be over, I can't take it!" Versus: "No! I have to outlast this! It will get better!"

Oddly, I forgot all about my fervent prayers to God years ago when my life began running more smoothly over time. The answer to my constant prayers of the past crept up on me because it wasn't an earth-shattering event, it was a slow evolution that happened in those moments when I let go of one more wrong thought and replaced it with a healthy one.

I never prayed for a big, exciting life. I prayed for normal and I got it. God was faithful. I did what I could. He did what I could not. My sense of feeling lost was the outcome of hanging on to old feelings that no longer served any purpose. Getting up and trying again and again was the difference between reaching my goal or a wasted life.

> ## Vital Sign
>
> **Pay attention. Your miracle will come in bits and pieces, not in a Hollywood moment- if you don't give up.**

As you do the work and make progress in your new life, don't stress out when you find yourself at a new level of peace. As paradoxical as it sounds, this is a normal thought for codependents. We generally don't know what to do with a quiet, stable life and will often jeopardize ourselves again, just to get back into chaos and dysfunction, where we know the territory.

If you are not comfortable with being comfortable, just know this is another symptom of an unhealthy mind. This too will be addressed later in the Guide.

On the other hand, it's easy to stay stuck in your mess forever. There are plenty of people out there doing just that and it's not hard to find if you're simply looking for someone to be miserable with. Many support groups are full of them. Their baggage is their life. Without the same old problems and stories, they wouldn't have anything to talk about.

I am all in favor of joining a good support group. Just be sure you are surrounding yourself with people who actually want to get better, and are not making their problem the basis of their social life.

My daughter, who has her own powerful story, became aware of this tendency early on. She depends on AA to help her maintain her sobriety. She also chooses to be with people who are engaged in the world while staying in the program, rather than letting the program become their life. The difference is huge.

My personal example of how my 'normal' life crept up on me is proof there is a future for you. You are here for a reason. You have gifts. You have already survived so much. Now it's time for you to get proactive, instead of fending off attacks from all sides. You are ready to grab hold of the life you've dreamt about, right?

Or have you lost your dreams? Even worse, are you so confused and depressed you can't even conjure up a dream to hold on to? If that's the case, it's time for you to reclaim them. Keep reading.

* * *

When I finally divorced the father of my children after twelve years, I moved into a home of my very own. I remember a deep feeling of being lost because I didn't even know what colors I liked, what music appealed to me...nothing. I had become an extension of him and never developed my own sense of self. It was a frightening realization but it started me on a scary yet interesting journey of exploration to find out who and what I was all about. I learned I had to go about it one topic at a time. At first I was actually fearful. Gradually, however, it became exciting to discover those things I was naturally drawn to. I began to fill in the blank places where my personality should have been all along.

Here's what lies ahead when you understand what you're dealing with:

- A new inner strength. As a result of committing to getting beyond the cycle of codependence and all that goes with it, you will find your balance.
- You will be calm in situations that used to leave you feeling out of place and inferior, your head literally spinning.
- You won't be weighed down by the heaviness of depression, guilt and shame.
- You won't seek out 'busy-ness' because you can't stand being alone with your own thoughts. This includes

controlling, fixing and rescuing.

- Eventually your sexuality will return in a healthy way.
- You will realize it's not too late to do those things you always secretly wanted to.
- You may even discover you are talented in ways you never dared dream about before.
- It's possible that for the first time in your life you will dare to even have a dream.
- Your self image will improve and you will attract healthy people.
- Because you have become mindful of how your thoughts have affected your bodily health, you will take action and the result will be a more vibrant physical self.
- Best of all, you will eventually use everything that has happened to you to help others. You will be able to spot those people in a room full of strangers because you have been them.

When you stop craving someone else's life; stop feeling lost in a sadness that can't be described, you will be on your way to being an authentic, whole person.

When your existence no longer revolves around someone else's happiness or validation, you will be free to truly live your own life.

When your energy is no longer used to control, appease and fix others, you will have less anger and feel fully alive.

What lies ahead for you is emotional freedom

The most important aspect of all this is you have the opportunity to stop the generational pattern of abuse you emerged from. You can be the one in your entire family history and its future who does this heroic thing. Imagine a time when your children's children take having a loving, calm upbringing for granted. Imagine that they are now the ones people you and I wanted to be like. It's an incredible gift to them and your ability to do it lies ahead of you. There's some hard work to be done first, but it is within your reach.

As anyone who has succeeded at something will tell you, goals are crucial. After all, how can you know you have arrived if you don't know where you're going?

Allow yourself to dream

In order to create your future, take a few minutes and give yourself the pleasure of envisioning what good things lay ahead for you. Sit quietly for a few minutes and let your imagination play. Yes, playing is uncomfortable for us codependent-types, but do it anyway. Then write a few sentences describing what a healthy, normal life would look like for you. No need to go into details and day to day strategies as to how you're going to get there. Just jot down your most basic concept of a better life.

If you honestly don't know, just understand this is normal for people in your situation. Allow yourself to dream. It doesn't have to be 'right' or an absolute. You aren't carving a plan into stone. You can come back, erase what you've written and put something totally different down later, if you choose. You are giving yourself permission to feel alive again. *This is what lies ahead.*

_____

_____

_____

_____

_____

_____

The hierarchy of enlightenment

Back when I was in the corporate world, there was some training we took having to do with how people learn. You may be familiar with it. It looked like this:

1. Doesn't know he doesn't know	2. Knows that he doesn't know
3. Doesn't know that he knows	4. Knows that he knows (enlightenment)

When thinking about what it takes for an overcomer to arrive at the point of being an authentic participant in life, this thought process floated up from memory. Here's the parallel:

1. We're too terrified and isolated to know there is anything else. We are simply victims. Lost in our fear, we have no idea there is another way.

2. We become aware that not everyone lives like this but we don't know what to do to change things. We only know we are miserable, hurting and lost. We feel different and ashamed. This knowledge makes our pain even more unbearable because now we know not everyone lives this way. We crave the illusive 'normal' we see in others.

3. We begin to seek help, to change our circumstances. Years may go by. We read, go to therapy, gain knowledge but our soul still feels trapped. In our head, we understand but we haven't undergone a real transformation. *This is where many people in therapy quit because now they have to change how they think and behave.*

4. Finally, our head and our spirit connect and we know there is a way out. We become more and more separated from our past hurts. We have overcome and are ready for the life we really want. We know that we know and we are ready to evolve in higher ways. We are free to become the authentic human beings we were meant to be. We choose to move into our new life.

This process took me decades. I didn't even know there was a process until I recently looked back and realized how perfectly an overcomer's work fits into the previous illustration.

Even when we get to level four, there is still so much more to be done because there are lies still playing out in our minds, though we may not consciously hear them. These destructive murmurings have become so ingrained, we aren't aware of them most of the time. Those lies are a part of our makeup. They are also the reason that in spite of some important victories, we still feel heavy inside. Remember, too those lies will wreak havoc with our health, as well.

Russell Crowe portrayed the late Nobel Peace Prize recipient John Nash in *A Beautiful Mind* who suffered from an extreme case of schizophrenia. It took him years of excruciating treatment to eventually accept that those people following him everyday weren't real. Yet this brilliant man had to maintain a constant vigil every single day of his life in order to keep his hard-earned sanity.

Your demons may still be with you on a daily basis, but just like Nash, you can expose them, thereby neutralizing any power they have over you if you are ready to do whatever is necessary.

I've included this chart on enlightenment because each one of us fits into it somewhere. We just may not know where yet. For instance, not knowing that you don't know is typical when a crazy, unsafe, rigid or chaotic life is all you have ever experienced. How could you possibly know there is anything else? That's why isolation becomes a handy tool for controlling you as a child or as an adult in a sick relationship. Those who are in control do not want you to talk about your problems for fear of being exposed.

To get to stage Four, you first have to understand lies have been created by those who had control over you to keep you in your place and to validate their own damaging behavior; whether they intended to or not isn't even important anymore.

Those of us who have any kind of awareness will be tuned in to our unconscious self-talk everyday. While others seem to go effortlessly through their normal lives, we are busy fighting off lies and old, destructive beliefs at every turn. Just as the recovering addict takes one day – one moment - at a time, so must we. In time lies can be stomped out of existence with truth. But first you have to know what the truth is.

TWO

LIES THAT HAVE KEPT YOU IN BONDAGE

"A lie told often enough becomes the truth."–Lenin

"If you do not know the truth, you cannot recognize the lie."
– Joyce Meyer

From here on, we'll be examining the lies that have kept you

from moving forward in life. If we don't blast each one wide open, you will always have them buzzing around in your head like flies and no matter how normal you make yourself appear on the outside, your mind and soul will be furiously swatting at these soul-sucking untruths, draining your much needed energy and keeping you in a state of mental, emotional and physical unhealthiness. There are hundreds of lies we buy into everyday. The following are what I consider to be the biggest, most common and most destructive.

Lie # 1: I'm crazy.

This is a real feeling in most codependents' minds, thus the title of the book. After all, everything you experienced in your early years kept you in a constant state of confusion. Now, just when you think that momentary feeling of lightness you experience can be trusted, someone will say or do some insignificant thing and you tumble down your rickety little ladder of well-being and smash into your old reality with a hard 'thud.' You realize you are still susceptible to manipulation. It takes next to nothing to knock you down a notch or two and days to get back up again. It's an exhausting way to live. But because you are used to the drill, you lay there for a while feeling the old pain, believing the old lie that says something is wrong with you. You feel that familiar shame, paralyzing fear and perhaps rage. Then after an hour, a day or a month, you pull your emotional self together, put all your people pleasing skills in high gear, and try again.

Just as debilitating is the opposite extreme. You are immobilized. You feel nothing except a dull, endless fatigue. When stuck in this state, it's impossible to get proactive and take charge. Isn't that what codependents do best: take charge, control and fix everything? If you can no longer do those things, you feel like you're losing your mind and your purpose. For example, you may go from detached to enraged over some minor occurrence then be filled with remorse. You learn not to trust your own thoughts and feelings. Believing something is wrong with you leads to insecurity. With that driving your life, you have a very hard time connecting with people because you judge them according to how much better they are than you – or how superior you are (we have to over estimate ourselves just to function in the world.) That is a frightening and exhausting way to exist.

When my mother got upset with me, she would just stop talking to me for days. Even after I had my own kids, there were many situations where this happened. I know now that this was her manipulative way of punishing me. The unspoken message I received as a child was: REJECTED. Nothing could have been more devastating. My head would spin like crazy for days trying to figure out ways to get her to like me again. Then, as if nothing had happened, because we did not discuss such things, everything went back to normal. Never knowing what would set her off left me feeling uncertain and anxious.

When my father would kiss me on the cheek one day and verbally denigrate me the next, I learned I could not depend on him. No matter how I tried, I couldn't get my father to love me consistently, which sent the message there was something wrong with me. At such a young age, I had no way of knowing it wasn't even about me.

When my first husband would disappear for an entire day and evening with an old high school girlfriend and later get outraged at me for having the gall to question his whereabouts, I felt crazy. But because I was so insecure, I couldn't speak up even though I was drowning in rage. So I sunk into depression and cried all day.

In all three scenarios, I wasn't the one behaving badly, yet somehow I was being punished. It made no sense. There is no easier way to slip into a mindset of not trusting your own innate senses than to have your reality turned upside down by someone else who is only interested in serving their own purposes. All of it boiled down to my ultimate, terrifying fear of abandonment. **This is the core of codependency**. If not confronted, it will drive a person crazy.

For a child, feeling responsible for keeping secrets, being too terrified to establish healthy boundaries, constantly seeking acceptance that never comes; or living in a perpetual state of confusion, forces him or her to deny their true feelings including unspeakable fear, anger and shame. Instead they learn to be 'nice' or compliant to stay safe. Since this coping mechanism provided protection early in life, as an adult he or she has no idea if their feelings are real or just learned reactions as a means to survive the harsh realities of life. Being out of touch with your feelings creates a sense of craziness because many times what you're feeling and how you behave in contrast to what is happening don't match up.

Another consequence of being raised in an unhealthy environment is generally known as Distortional Thinking, which psychiatrist Dr. Aaron Beck first called "automatic thoughts." People with this problem can't see a gray area. It's all or nothing; black or white. They are easily defeated because if one thing goes wrong, they throw their hands up in the belief that everything else will go wrong, too. They see the world through a negativity which cannot be broken. Good is discounted. Either they minimize situations that really are important or they magnify others which aren't. They live by their feelings rather than using good judgment. They are quick to label and judge everyone, especially themselves (notice how many times in a conversation you say things like, "I'm such an idiot.") Finally, whatever does go wrong is somehow always their fault.

Becoming skilled at an early age not to feel, and learning to depend on distortional thinking to guide you through life will definitely leave you feeling crazy.

Write down how this lie has affected your life

_____

_____

_____

_____

_____

_____

_____

_____

Truth # 1
Your environment was crazy, not you.

Earlier in this book, I described my upbringing. Did it sound healthy and stable to you? Of course not. I was born into an emotional super storm. I understand all the whys now but back then those reasons didn't matter when I was trying to scratch my dad's eyes out, or crying in the dark because I felt so rejected by my own parents. I had child-like innocence. My environment was absolutely crazy.

Children don't realize that what they are experiencing is insane because it is all they know. How could you have possibly known that other kids weren't being beaten, rejected, hounded and berated twenty four hours a day? Do you remember feeling terrified and ashamed that someone might find out what awful things were going on in your household? I can't think of any adult who could live under those circumstances and not eventually go crazy, too.

I was not allowed to talk back or debate the continual criticism and non-stop nagging that filled my days. All of my emotions were relegated to my head until I got older and started to take my father on physically. It was no wonder when I finally got the heck out of there, I was about as unstable as a two legged chair. But of course, I didn't know it. No surprise then, that every decision I made the minute I walked out was formulated not out of a calm, rational process but out of desperation and impulsive feelings. Disaster after disaster was the result.

Thinking you're crazy or something is wrong with you is nothing but a lie to keep you in your cage. This cage was created years ago as means to control you by someone who had authority over you, even if it wasn't intentional. This could have been done with verbal, physical, emotional even sexual abuse.

Remember, emotional abuse can be administered invisibly. Withholding of affection, ignoring, and the absence of interaction all send the frightening message to children that they are unimportant. Something must be wrong with them; otherwise why would their own parents not want to be with them? It's a crushingly sad sight when a little boy or girl tries everything they know – including acting out or feigning sickness – just to get someone to pay attention to them. Perhaps addiction was dragging your parents away. Whatever the reason, it was emotional abuse or neglect.

'Crazy' as used here is not the equivalent of insane. While most codependents are doing the best they can to cope with the junk they were saddled with from their erratic past, they are functioning. Insane people cannot function. Insane people do not know wrong from right. You do. You know there is something better out there. You know how you are living is suffocating your spirit. You know you are not satisfied and want simple things like calm and stability in your life. This isn't crazy; it's innately human.

Undoing your earlier programming and allowing your true feelings to be heard may take some time. You won't trust them at first because you will feel vulnerable. By being willing to feel, you open yourself up to some things that will hurt. You will survive it. Instead of using false emotions to build walls for protection, you'll begin to let authentic feelings come through. Be patient with yourself as you may overreact from time to time. Feelings are powerful. "Getting in touch with your feelings" isn't just a cliché; it's a priority if you are ever going to have a sense of truly alive.

As for the distortional thinking, there are many therapists trained to help you become aware of your thinking as well as books and CD's available to help you to gradually change. The

first step is to be aware of how you think, and then start to turn it around. There is much more discussion about this in the Guide.
The first lie has been exposed.

Lie # 2
It's too hard.

In my introduction I wrote there is no hierarchy of pain. There are people who went through much worse than you or me and lived victoriously. Conversely, there are people who went through far less and failed to thrive their entire lives.

Grappling with codependency and dealing with all sorts of pain is undeniably difficult. But you are not alone. See if you relate to any of the following.

You left an unhappy, unloving home only to jump from one turbulent relationship to another. You have made one bad choice after another with disastrous consequences. You can't seem to see things like school or careers through to the finish. You have a hard time getting along with people. Everyone wants too much from you but you can't say 'no'. You're depleted, depressed, angry and feel hopeless.

You've spent your entire life – consciously or unconsciously - creating your current persona. In the process you have taken on perfectionist tendencies, are highly controlling and have developed a hyper vigilance; a keen awareness when anything threatens to take you out of your comfort zone. You are on twenty-four hour guard because you learned early you had to be or you could get hurt. You have the uncanny ability to morph into whatever type of person you think others expect you to be, which leaves you feeling empty, resentful and worn out. In spite of all your work to be just right, you have terrible self esteem and are terrified someone will find out what a fraud you are.

Or, perhaps you came from an environment where you were loved but were expected to be perfect in every way. You had to look just right. This is particularly devastating to young girls: weight, skin, clothes are all the source of your approval. You had to excel in school, sports, popularity, etc. When you did, you were adored and showered with accolades. When you didn't you were criticized and compared with others. Thus began the cycle of people pleasing and perfectionism.

All roads lead to becoming hyper-controlling. You have lost your spontaneity, your ability to relax, are plagued with guilt, can't enjoy yourself; and above all you do not trust anyone. You are overworked, overwhelmed and feel there is never enough time to get everything done. All of these attributes are part of your survival kit. To lower your protective shield even for a second could be disastrous. *Notice again how some of the symptoms taken from Dr. Levine's book on trauma run parallel to those of codependency.*

The very concept of changing how you approach life is confusing and hard. It's especially tough when you've lost the ability to see a bright future and really can't envision yourself being different than you are right now.

The lie that 'it's too hard' confirms your fear you can never be anything other than what you are. You can never have a better life than you what you're enduring now. Deep inside you believe you are not good enough and never will be. It's likely the people you are trying so hard to please all the time reinforce this notion to keep you in your place, even as an adult. What's more, if you change, those same people might not want you anymore. Surely, you couldn't survive that.

If you see yourself in any or all of the above, let me ask you: isn't it hard to maintain this kind of vigilance? Aren't you sick and tired of living your life for the sole purpose of making sure you aren't rejected or abandoned? Aren't you just a little worn out from believing you have to control everything and be all things to all people?

Remember, you have been at this endless job since you were little. Back then, you tried everything you knew to get your parents to love and accept you. When that didn't happen, your little mind was constantly at work, trying to understand why; struggling to cope with some pretty powerful emotions with no help from anyone else.

You have been running in a race you know you will never win as far back as you can remember but don't know how to stop. It's possible the cost of all that running is manifesting in physical ailments you have to also contend with now. You might be good at making all this hard work seem easy on the outside, but it's taking its toll inside. For anyone living in this frantic, endless cycle life definitely *is* too hard. But it doesn't have to be.

Write down how this lie has affected your life.

_____

_____

_____

_____

_____

_____

Truth # 2
Dying without ever having lived is harder.

We're all going to die. I don't want to be on my deathbed wishing I had done the work so I could have had a better life. To experience real peace and contentment even for a short time would have been worth every moment of effort.

Back in the mid-seventies, I had the profound opportunity to meet the now deceased Dr. Elisabeth Kubler-Ross. She had written a groundbreaking book in 1969 entitled, *On Death and*

Dying, and was the keynote speaker at a conference I had helped organize on Holistic Health long before most of our country knew what those words meant. When we get to the Guide portion of this book, you'll understand why they are now important to you. Her work identified for the first time the 'Five Stages of Grief' people usually go through upon facing death. They are:

1. Denial – "I'm fine." "This isn't happening to me."
2. Anger – "Why me? "It's not fair!"
3. Bargaining – "I'll do anything if…."
4. Depression – "What's the point of going on…."
5. Acceptance – "It's going to be okay."

Years later these stages came be applied to any form of catastrophic event or trauma, *including addiction.* Earlier, I had compared the traits of codependency to addiction.

This is why these stages are important in understanding the truth about the lie 'It's too hard.' Just as addicts go through these phases before conceding they are powerless to change, codependent people must come to the same realization. The way you have been functioning, thinking, reacting, talking and surviving are all based in something that has in reality kept you powerless to become a healthy, well-adjusted person.

Denial

You may have been in denial that you even had a problem your whole life. A lot of people think their rotten disposition, bad temper, terrible social skills are all just family traits that are in their blood and there isn't anything they can do about it. Excuses such as, "Everyone in my family is controlling, I can't help it" are just that: excuses and lies.

Another form of denial when someone says, "It's not my fault! I can't help it." On one hand they are deceiving themselves but on the other they are displaying a learned helplessness.

This is also a characteristic of being codependent. If your partner expects to control you, it's imperative that you learn to be helpless for the arrangement to work.

Vital Sign

Healing begins
when events that have been denied are exposed

Trauma victims use denial as a way to survive, as related earlier by Dr. Levine. "This isn't happening" allows the brain to shut down and not feel the experience. Working through the terrible things that happened to you will no doubt create moments of denial. Minimizing those events as you recall them is a form of this.

Facing the truth is hard. But it is the first step in your recovery. You must be willing to feel the pain of remembering. You must work through any denial that those things happened or are still happening to you. Once you do, anger will take the place of denial and will consume you if you aren't mindful.

Anger

I was angry all the time. It took work for me not be upset even when my life in the moment was peaceful. Anger was part of who I was. Without even really thinking about it, my inner self was constantly upset about things that had happened which I had not healed from: lost opportunities, wrong choices, guilt and the belief that I was helpless to change anything, especially myself. I remember walking down dark streets after work in the city hoping somebody would get in my way so I would have a reason to get into a fight. I was always looking for an outlet for my rage. In a way, it was better than being frightened all the time, but absolutely exhausting, not to mention potentially dangerous.

At the other extreme, I have met people who cannot feel any anger in spite of the terrible wrongs done to them. They had shut down emotionally. Instead, they became intellectual about their situation. They rationalized to the point of being obsessive. And because they were so terribly codependent, instead of concentrating on healing themselves, they ruminated over and over on how to fix the very people or person who hurt them. This is a crazy maker and another core attribute of codependency.

Anger is good. You must be in touch with all your emotions to be fully alive. It's not good to let it run your life. In the Guide, we will discuss appropriate ways to express and alleviate anger.

Bargaining

Further down the road of recovery, you will want to bargain with God or whatever power you trust. "If you just give me the strength to stand my ground so I can end this terrible relationship, I promise I will......" It's interesting that many codependents do not worship any particular god. But as the saying goes: "There are no atheists in a foxhole." When you are in a battle for your life, this axiom takes on a whole new perspective.   Recently I heard someone give a sermon on arrogance. One sentence stuck in my mind because of this chapter. He said it is arrogant to bargain with God instead of trusting Him. This gets right to the heart of the matter.

Depression

From there you will move on to depression, unless you have been struggling with it your whole life, as I did. It's possible to experience both (new and ongoing). There are at least 15 types of depression. For our purposes, we'll refer to these three:

1. Clinical or major depression – episodes which occur off

and on throughout life and last for at least two weeks at a time.

2. Dysthymia – chronic, mild form which creates a nearly constant depressed mood for at least two years at a time.

3. Situational - a response to stressful occurrences (death, trauma, divorce, etc.) and usually only lasts up to six months.

Again, it is completely possible to struggle with a constant depressed mood almost every day and get hit with a second Situational Depression when a major, disturbing event rocks your world. If you have been depressed for as long as you can remember, you are not fully alive and need to get help. If you aren't sure what you're feeling, here are the basic symptoms of depression:

- persistent sad, anxious or 'empty' mood
- feelings of hopelessness, pessimism
- feelings of guilt, worthlessness, helplessness
- loss of interest or pleasure in things you once enjoyed
- decreased energy, fatigue, feeling 'slowed down'
- difficulty concentrating, remembering or making decisions
- difficulty sleeping or sleeping too much
- change in appetite, sudden weight loss or gain
- thoughts of death and/or suicide; suicide attempts
- restless, irritable
- persistent physical symptoms that don't respond to treatment

Acknowledging you might be suffering from this disease is a step in the right direction. How to treat depression will be discussed in the Guide.

Acceptance

Finally you will get to the point of Acceptance. "It happened. It was awful and unfair but I accept it and can now start healing." This means you have worked your way all the way through the process beginning with denial.

The other important fact you will come to accept is that control is no longer your sole purpose in life. Accepting you cannot change the people who hurt you or what happened is one of the most liberating aspects to overcoming codependency.

Only you will know when it's time to take that step. Acceptance is not to be confused with forgiveness. We will address that later.

The reason I have spelled this information out is to help you understand what to expect. I've found that knowing what's coming, while scary, isn't nearly as hard as being sucker-punched by life again and again. Anything worth having is definitely going to be hard.

Most codependents unwittingly surround themselves with people who don't validate them on any level. So let me ask you, has anyone told you how strong you are lately? Probably not. This is another form of emotional abuse and manipulation. But to you it seems normal.

Consider this: you have made it to this point with only your wits and sheer determination. Even if you can't see it yet, you are strong and a survivor. You've already been through a multitude of hard times.

If the unthinkable should happen and you find yourself facing your own mortality in the near future, will you have regret that you did nothing to reach for a better life? I can't think of anything harder to face than the awful truth that I was afraid to try.

Lie # 3
It's too late.

For decades I felt inferior because I didn't have my college degree. I ached when I heard my younger sibling go on and on about funny college experiences. I wanted that so badly, but my time had come and gone. One more thing to feel bad about.

In 2003 I took an art class at a local junior college, then another. I began to toy with the idea of going back to school. Even though it was an exhilarating thought, I didn't believe it was in the cards for me. Fortunately, I am now married to a wonderful man who greatly values education, having a PhD. himself. The time had come when it was a financial possibility so I jumped in. It took me four decades, but I finally received my Bachelors Degree in 2007. It was bittersweet because as the 'old lady' in the classroom I didn't have the typical college experience. But I did meet a goal. I got my degree. I look at the diploma hanging in the office behind me as I write and it serves as a reminder that it is never too late.

By the way, the entire time I was in college, I had a picture taped to my bathroom mirror of a silver haired woman whose name is gone from me now, who made the news because she received her degree at the age of ninety-three. Every morning I would look at her picture and think, if she could do it, then so can I. If it wasn't too late for her at age 93, then it wasn't too late for me either.

Here's my point: time goes by. We get a little more tired and set in our ways each year. If no one is affirming you and you are spending all your energy seeing to it that everyone else's dreams come true at the expense of your own, then it may seem like it's too late for you to change, have a happier life or even start over.

There are practical concerns; maybe there's not enough money, time or energy for you to take a life changing step in a new direction right now. Besides, it's much easier to keep fixing other people's problems, obsess over whether you have the world under control and complain about your fate.

The lie wants to keep you stuck. Don't count on the very people who filled your head up with lies as a child, to support you now that you are determined to get well.

When I was cowering on the floor with the guy from college screaming at me saying no one would ever want me but him while he slapped me around, I believed him because it was consistent with what I heard growing up. I was too young and terrified to know I could speak up, all I felt was paralyzing fear and confusion. Besides, I learned a long time ago talking back just brought on more trouble.

When I knew I had to divorce my ex-husband and reached out for support from my mother, she promptly told me nobody else would want me and I'd better hang to what I had. Thank God by then, even in my frazzled state I knew that was a lie. It only made me determined to prove her wrong. Anger has its uses.

The people you are always rescuing and fixing have a vested interested in keeping you the same. When you are lost in someone else's problems, they don't have to take responsibility and you don't have to face your own shortcomings. Years go by and nothing changes. In fact, you will have passed your habits on to your children. Any dreams you once had will quietly disappear.

As children you and I had no choice but to hear and believe the lies we were told every day. We knew nothing else, so we accepted them as truth. From there, as was my case, we fall right into other destructive relationships where we are constantly berated, ignored, manipulated and even abused. At this point in your life, you must question everything you accepted as real or the truth. Allow yourself to see your life a year from now. What will be different? The answer is *nothing* if you continue to believe this lie.

Write down how this lie has affected your life.

_____

_____

_____

_____

_____

_____

Truth # 3
Time is going to go by anyway.
Make it work for you.

When I looked at that woman's picture on my mirror, I would see myself and think, "You know, in four years you're going to be fifty-five whether you get this degree or not. If you don't do this now, you'll still be wishing and whining or you could have a party." I chose the party.

It wasn't easy. I felt incredibly awkward in every classroom. I wanted to smack those silly, young know-it-alls. In some classes I knew more than the teachers. In others I felt like a complete idiot, like the Algebra classes I was required to take where I felt humiliated when I held things up because of my dumb questions.

In addition, I still had a daughter at home who was going through her own hard time. My new marriage was sputtering. I was trying to get a real estate business off the ground in the town we had recently moved to. I was heavily involved in a volunteer position requiring a lot of time and energy. I was tired, emotional, overworked and lest we forget, still dealing with a lot of stuff from my past which was keeping me from coping as well as I could have. And of course, I didn't listen to my body because I believed I should be able to do it all! Classic stuff of the codependent.

I wanted to give up many times. But the truth was I loved learning and it was a good escape. I did well in school. Even though the time for me to need a college degree to make my way in the world had passed - another casualty of lost time - I wanted it so I kept moving forward. As a result, I have the satisfaction of finally finishing something I walked away from so long ago.

My kids see my accomplishment as inspirational. "Mom did that? Then I can do this." I may not have had the typical college experience but I did what I could.

This is a rather superficial example of determination in my life, but there were lots of life-altering ones. For instance, I bought a one-way train ticket out of the state where that abusive man from college was, even though he threatened to find me. I began seeking help because I suffered from depression. I learned how my past was affecting my present. I made more mistakes but kept going even when I didn't think I could get up again. Eventually, I got strong enough to speak up when others hurt or took advantage of me. I found good role models because I hadn't grown up with any. In short, I didn't stop. I screwed up at times, and I beat myself up for it, but eventually I made things right. I still wake up each day and have to make a conscious decision to think and behave in a healthy manner and not revert to old, habitual habits.

You can do what you need to also when you decide to heal from your past. Maybe years, even decades have gone by and you are resentful or just plain sad about something you haven't been able to accomplish. It could be as noble as healing from your past, developing healthy coping methods, getting sober, breaking the mindset of codependency, a new career, relocation; even divorce. It could be as simple as deciding to become aware of and end the habit of negative self-talk which is not as easy as it sounds.

It's not too late unless you quit trying. Once you give up, you are condemning yourself to a self-inflicted lost life. But when you grasp the concept that you are in a battle for a better future and you are not going to give in to the lies of your past, you then have time on your side. Just as with me and the degree – you will be a year older next year, God willing. Are you going to still be stuck in neutral or are you going to get moving and claim the life you were intended to have?

Take an honest look at the way you spend your time. A day in the life of a typical codependent is filled with being over-whelmed, because it presents a feeling of worthiness (look how hard I work), controlling, fixing or rescuing other people who could probably handle their stuff on their own given the opportunity, worrying, turning cartwheels to impress people who you desperately want approval from and, of course, exhaustion. It's hard being codependent!

There is another red flag that goes along with letting time slip by. Your health is at stake. Codependency is the result of dysfunction you lived with in childhood, in most cases. That being the case, you had continual 'fight or flight' adrenal overload from an early age. Being peaceful does not come easy for the codependent personality. When a body is in constant stress mode, it gets worn down. Sickness finds its way in much easier as explained earlier.

If smoking, drinking and other unhealthy coping mechanisms have been helping you get through your days, that's extra wear and tear on your internal organs. In many cases, codependents are so busy taking care of others, they neglect their own bodies. Years may go by with no exercise or attention to stress levels. Eating habits are less than ideal because the mind is never relaxed and able to enjoy a meal. Shoveling something into your mouth while a constant stream of anxious thoughts flood your mind is not going to provide the nourishment you need to stay healthy.

There is also growing evidence that a lifetime of stress

actually encourages cancer and other devastating diseases to attack the body. Having lost several friends to various forms of cancer, I have a reverential fear of letting stress steal my health.

Anger, trauma, anxiety, fear and other negative aspects of your past that have not been worked through can take a terrible toll on your body. Time can be your friend or your enemy. Choose wisely.

Lie #4
I'm not worthy.

This is the mother of all lies and one of the scariest because it's so subliminal. Although you may not have ever said, "I am not worthy," you feel it in your bones. You know you're a fraud and hope to get through each day hoping no one will figure it out. It's impossible to imagine how many miracles have gone undiscovered, great works left untried and lives not fully lived due to the power of this evil concept.

You don't have to be a psychiatrist to know that if you have been told your whole life you are stupid, worthless, ugly, lazy or not as wonderful as someone else, you will grow into an adult with those wrong thoughts firmly embedded in your psyche. If you were ignored; if your basic need for nurturing was not met, you no doubt feel unworthy at some level.

If you experienced shaming abuse (sexual, verbal or other form of dysfunction that required secrecy, creating a perverse sense of guilt), or constant criticism for just being who you were, this lie is part of your DNA. When there is shame, there is also the innate belief that one is not worthy of respect. Revisit Part One where I asked you to write about how you felt about yourself. All those negative adjectives affirm this bold-face lie.

Reinforcement of these toxic affirmations comes again and again, as you are repeatedly drawn to partners who treat you exactly the way you unconsciously believe you deserve: badly. If you don't even have the awareness that only you can turn this cycle around, you are doomed to a miserable, self-fulfilling prophecy of disastrous, unfulfilling relationships leaving you void of true intimacy and peace.

The poor choices you make due to the fundamentally flawed belief that you don't deserve to enjoy a full, healthy life may create outcomes which heap piles of additional condemnation on you. The guilt, shame, resentment, fear and insecurity you carry all bear themselves out in how you choose to function in the world.

In addition, the potential for greatness which has always been within you will also remain hostage to this lie, leaving all your gifts such as creativity, unopened. This is a tragedy for everyone.

When you believe you are unworthy or inferior and not strong enough to change, you are right where those who want control over you to be: immobile, insecure and non- threatening.

Most often this type of damage was done early in life by those responsible for your safety – usually parents. In some cases, it happened later in relationships with people who for whatever reasons felt a need to control you – and you let them.

What does any of this have to do with being codependent? It created the framework in your mind that in order to be loved, you had the impossible task of trying to extract love and approval from people who either could not or would not give those things to you. As a result, you grew into a highly controlling person as you constantly tried to create a scenario that would make you acceptable.

As a chronic overachiever, you've run in circles trying to be the best at everything, always feeling like it wasn't enough. You became a people pleaser with poor boundaries; again, because you were starved for some sign of approval. Most likely, you chose relationships based in your trying to 'fix' or appease the other person while your own needs went unmet. Often times your partner struggled with one form of addiction or another, but many of you understood this lifestyle because you grew up with it. Enabling, fixing, fighting, and self-neglect were all modeled for you as a child. It's what you're good at.

Years can slip by as you fight the losing, overwhelming battle to control everyone and everything around you all with the deep seated knowledge that you are secretly completely out of control. It's an exhausting way to survive. Never the less, it's still easier to work at changing the world than it is to stop and do an honest evaluation of yourself. That would be terrifying.

Your unrelenting efforts to create a rigid, false but seemingly perfect and thereby acceptable presence on the outside is all an attempt to cover up the idea you bought into a long time ago. You are not good enough. You are not worthy. You are codependent.

Write down how this lie has affected your life

_____

_____

_____

_____

_____

_____

_____

Truth #4
If God is for us, who can be against us?

I realize when you are hurting having Bible verses handed to you may not be what you ache for. At least that's how it felt for me. I wanted real life answers! Yet, eventually I learned – the hard way of course - that to really understand just how evil **Lie #4** is, I had to be beaten down to my knees. Completely out of energy, answers and hope; after years of looking in all the wrong places, I was ready to hear the truth.

At the time, I was married to a man who was a narcissist and a workaholic. I felt angry, abandoned and depressed. I was sick constantly. To be fair, dealing with all those issues didn't make me a very desirable wife, I'm sure. My two little girls just wanted their mommy, but ironically, most of the time I was drained from trying to keep what others perceived to be the perfect family together to really enjoy them. It was overwhelming.

Finally, after being asked many times, I accepted a friend's invitation to go to the Episcopal Church where my girls' preschool was. Upon entering the little sanctuary, I literally felt the Holy Spirit all around me. I began attending regularly and cried every Sunday for a year. Not because I was sad, although I certainly was, but because I felt I had finally come home. I found what was missing in my life. That realization started a spiritual journey for me which continues today.

There are a couple of things I am grateful to my mother for. One is for insisting on good table manners. The other is for dragging us to that Lutheran Church in my youth because it provided a directional sign to find 'home' when I needed it most.

Romans 8:31 rebukes the lie 'you are not worthy'. If God is for you, then who cares what lies other people have drilled into your head? I encourage you to find a Bible and read all of Romans 8 for starters. It states in no uncertain terms nothing can keep us from the love of God. How about that. Not the lies you were told, not the poor choices you made because you weren't given a proper set of decision-making tools, not your lousy self-image or any of the negative thoughts you obsess about can keep you from the love of God. He doesn't care if you're perfect (unattainable anyway), so you can relax.

I don't expect everyone reading this to simply accept my belief. I am a Christian, but I didn't come to my decision easily. True, I was raised in the Lutheran Church but back then it was just part of a routine intended to keep stability in an otherwise chaotic home. Once I left, I walked away from everything, including religion. Young, hurting and lost, I never even considered going to church because it was nothing more to me than an obligation. I was a seeker however, and looked for truth in more exotic places such as a Hari Krishna temple, the I Ching, spirit guides, Eastern religions…you name it.

Later I read books by C.S. Lewis, scholar, writer and creator of the Narnia series. He was also raised Christian and after much intellectual rationalization, chose to become an atheist. In one of his many books, "*A Case for the Christian Faith,*" he wrote that after years of searching, the Truth was revealed to him while sitting on a double-decker bus. Soon after, he got on his knees and gave his life to Christ. His logical approach to understanding Christianity, and his ultimate decision to bow down and accept Christ in faith was good enough for me.

His work appealed to my hunger for rational evidence, because codependents absolutely thrive on reasoning and rationalizing. I decided to reclaim my Christian upbringing and to make it an essential part of my life, rather than a duty to be performed once a week. Admittedly, my faith is strong at some times and invisible at others. I work on it daily.

I believe I was created by God and He loves me. No matter how unlovable I feel, He still loves me. My past experiences taught me the world could not be trusted, but I eventually learned God is always faithful. Yes, one of the gifts He gives us is free choice and those who abused and neglected you and me used that freedom badly. But that was them at work, not Him. Free choice is a gift mankind has misused in every conceivable way since the beginning.

In everything I have read about other Western and Eastern religions, nowhere did I see a God who does not love His children. "God Is Love" is the universal, common thread in most religions. **This is not about choosing a religion, but rather a relationship.**

It is about understanding that the world, and all the broken people in it, pale in comparison to the love of our maker. Nothing can keep you from the love of God. To not allow this concept into your life leaves a hole I don't believe anything else can fill.

If you are Christian, it's very possible it has been twisted into a tool and used against you. A vengeful, hateful, punishing God is a powerful weapon in manipulating a person into perpetual bondage and shame. That's tragic.

I have a dear friend who has been in recovery from alcoholism for sixteen years. Unfortunately, she was raised by Catholic extremists who were unspeakably cruel to her. Attending AA was out of the question for her as she sought out help from her addiction because she could not bring herself to acknowledge a higher power. Fortunately, she found a program through a local hospital which worked for her. She is still mad at God, but because she admits she is still arguing with Him, instead of denying His existence, I believe one day there will be reconciliation.

I recognize my point of view isn't going to be for everyone. Some of you aren't open to having a relationship with God – that's your choice. For your sake, though, I hope you believe in something larger than yourself to help reclaim your life. Remember, the people you are trying to keep happy don't want you to change or feel empowered.

If you are going to break out of the cage you've been locked in all your life, you must look beyond what you can see. This is called faith.

There is another benefit to recognizing you are loved by God. You will open up an untapped power source within you. It's always been there, you just didn't know it.

"For I know the plans I have for you, declares the Lord. They are plans for good and not disaster, to give you hope and a future. In those days when you pray I will listen. If you look for me in earnest, you will find me." (Jeremiah 29:11)

This means you, Beloved, are worthy of all good things.

* * *

Take a moment and let the possibility of those words sink in. Give yourself permission to imagine a life not loaded down with the heaviness of feeling so unworthy. Does the idea that you are loved just the way you are and always have been, feel somehow foreign? In spite of everything - the shameful things done to you, or what you have done; the awful things you believe about yourself or what others may have drilled into your brain - you are still loved. It's almost too much to take in. But it's true.

By understanding **Truth #4**, you now have two powerful pieces of ammunition to help you win your daily battles against codependency and all that goes with it.

- You are lovable just the way you are by God and always have been.
- You have within you His power to overcome anything standing in the way as you work toward becoming the stable, peaceful, creative and whole person you were meant to be.

Lie # 5
I'll never be able to forgive them for what they did to me.

This is certainly a justified feeling. When you remember what you've gone through at the hands of other people, you have the right to feel hurt and even enraged. Newspapers are dotted with horror stories of despicable things parents do to their children. We read them and think, "That's absolutely unforgivable."

People may wonder how in the world you ever survived such abuse and still function as well as you do. But then, this is one of the hallmarks of the codependent: we make it look easy on the outside even if we are aching and crazed on the inside.

Most codependents don't come from horrendous, front-page type backgrounds. My own story may pale in comparison to what you experienced. Still, most angry, anxiety-riddled, depressed, addicted, ailing codependents have background commonalities which include verbal, emotional, physical or sexual abuse at one degree or another. Some had to deal with addicted parents, trauma and of course, lots of shame. Refer back to the beginning of the book where we discussed the pieces of the Puzzle called Codependency. Remember, most of us were raised by people who were themselves either codependent, abused or caught up in the web of addiction and/or dysfunction on some level. Statistically, most of them were raised with it in one way or another. Remember, it's generational.

It's not necessarily the extremes of these occurrences, but the consistency that did the damage. Even if you don't remember what happened, the routine of a troubled, sick upbringing will create patterns of thinking which are still very real to you decades later.

It's possible the most powerfully damaging occurrences contributing to you becoming codependent looked innocent to the world: the lack of nurturing, the absence of affection or withholding of acknowledgment. Being made to feel responsible for things you didn't even understand at too young an age because

95

the adults were out of control due to addiction, emotional instability, etc., is also a cruel burden to put on a child.

Today your life is still a mess because of things that happened to you as far back as infancy or as recent as ten minutes ago. People continue to manipulate, abuse and neglect you, and in the process steal any chance you have of feeling normal. It's understandable that knowing this makes you want to hurt somebody besides yourself, which you manage to do regularly one way or the other. And then there is the damage you pass on to your children.

When you think about the lost opportunities, the premature aging, the physical problems you have developed due to endless stress, the loss of your innocence, the nagging sense you are somehow guilty no matter what happens ...not to mention the obvious: you are cursed with the characteristics of being codependent, how do you forgive people who were supposed to protect you but instead saddled you with all these problems?

Being a victim of abuse or neglect is a profound position for anyone to end up in. For the codependent, it's especially difficult because in addition to being the victim, we also believe we have the burden of being responsible for keeping the very people who hurt us happy in whatever twisted dynamic each family embraces.

The adult child, wounded as she is, still feels she needs to keep her manipulative mother appeased, lest she lose her approval...again. The grown man is afraid to confront his alcoholic father for fear of rejection or attack. The battered or neglected wife continues to put up with her cruel husband because she is thoroughly convinced, thanks to his endless rants that no one else would ever want her. Or she goes under the knife again and again to attain the perfect body for a man who thinks of her as a trophy he can show off.

It's possible you feel guilty trying to forgive when the

forms of dysfunction put on you were so subtle yet consistent, you're not sure you really were abused. Forgiveness seems like a distant, unimportant word when faced with these daily realities.

Then there is the hardest job of all. How can you ever forgive yourself? After all, you are full of dirty secrets and hateful, negative thoughts. You were forced to do things you cannot talk about because they are so awful. You may have then later chosen to act out in ways you are deeply ashamed of. Perhaps the saddest fact is you are letting your life slip away because you are too scared, angry or exhausted to make those big changes which involve facing your demons.

Finally, you continue to let those people who suffocated your true self treat you with disrespect because you're too insecure to face them. The fear of abandonment, even from those who still hurt you, runs deep. Saying 'no' isn't something you're good at.

Everything you have gone through has left you with codependent traits that have run your life and continue to sabotage your daily existence. You aren't just a victim of past wrong doings. Your very being is the culmination of those events. You are not a complete, healthy person. You have a perverted sense of yourself. Your true being never had a chance in light of the way you were forced to live and because of the regular messages you received; all of which said that somehow you weren't lovable. Codependency has had a field day with your life. Considering all this, forgiving will be an enormous job. Is it even possible or necessary?

Write down how this lie has affected your life

_____

_____

_____

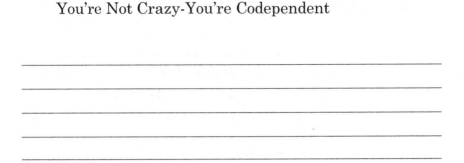

Truth # 5
Forgiveness of others is possible eventually.
Forgiveness of ourselves is required
to be fully alive.

The primary thing to understand about forgiveness is that it is the last step in healing, not the first. The second fact is – and this is difficult –for some people and situations, it may feel as though it is just not possible at the moment.

This contradicts all the Christian values I was raised with. I was taught that in order to have peace on this earth, we must forgive, just as we have been forgiven. It's part of the Lord's Prayer, for heaven's sake.

I believe if we are ever going to make peace with the past and all the events and people who hurt us we absolutely must get to the point where we can forgive. Remember, I said it would not be a one-time event. Forgiveness usually comes in the form of a daily, yearly sometimes even hourly exercise. We have to forgive over and over – and mean it even though we won't feel any different at first. It takes time. This is where having faith comes in handy. Doing it without the help of God is – I believe – not possible.

I also don't believe the old adage 'forgive and forget' applies to situations such as those the codependent has gone through because it's not a matter of forgetting. What happened made us who we are. How can we forget that? We can't. We can forgive and *let go* eventually. I realize it sounds like a bumper sticker, but it's true.

When I say 'let go' I mean we *release ourselves* from the *bondage* those beliefs and events held us in for so long. That comes through dedicated work, prayer, learning, therapy and sometimes the use of medication to help us get past the pain so we can instead focus on the core issues. When we finally understand we really can neutralize the effects of those beliefs and events, we gain a power no one can take from us. Exposing some of the lies we have bought into, which is what this book does, is part of the work.

To forgive means we understand those who hurt us were hurting, too. This is not meant to make excuses. They were utterly wrong. The over-arching fact though, is the reasons don't matter anymore. It simply stops being important to us to understand why. Our focus instead is on our own healing.

Speaking for myself, there came a time when I just got sick and tired –bored really - of feeling like a victim. I wanted my life on my terms. To do that, I had to release myself from all holds the past and present problematic relationships had on me. I slowly realized that if I hung on to anger, resentment even hatred, I would never be free to live my own life. If I went on acting and thinking like a frightened little girl, terrified of rejection, I would never have any personal power. I knew if I didn't kill the 'beast,' it was going to kill me.

I chose to forgive not to make certain people feel better. Quite the opposite; I never even told them. I did it for me.

Forgiving doesn't mean you have to stage a big scene with confrontation, emotion and a tearful dramatic finale. It just means you pray for the strength to forgive them so you can be free of all that pain at last. Over and over, you speak forgiveness - quietly. One day you notice your chest isn't quite as constricted. Your heart doesn't beat faster when you think of them. You don't feel the old anxiety when triggers pop up that reminds you of the past.

You don't have to constantly tell yourself to breathe. You are making progress and are on your way to being in charge of your life for the first time. It does not mean you cave and let people who are treating you badly in the present continue in the name of having forgiven them. That's not forgiveness, its concession which is an easy trap for people with weak boundaries to fall into. Watch yourself.

Step Nine of the 12-Step Program asks you to make amends with people *you* have harmed. That is *not* what we are talking about here. You were the victim, not the perpetrator. You may never talk to the people you want to forgive. This is for your benefit only. It has nothing to do with making anyone else feel better but you. Do it the way it works best for your own well-being. In this situation, your choosing to forgive isn't to reconcile a relationship. It's strictly for your own peace of mind.

Keep in mind it is entirely possible that even though you forgive someone, you may still never be able to have a relationship with that person in order to protect your health on all levels. *Building bridges isn't the goal here. Freedom from non-forgiveness and all that goes with it is.* When the time comes that you do want to go through a Twelve Step program for other reasons, by all means do it.

In fairness, I have to acknowledge that although pain is pain, what creates it has a spectrum. On the far side of that spectrum is a hurt I can't even imagine. Who am I to tell someone who has been through so much worse than me they need to forgive their perpetrators immediately, especially if those people were the very ones who were supposed to love and protect them? I can't.

With that realization, I must accept the idea that in some cases forgiveness, although a noble concept, may not be attainable *for now.* If you are one of these people, my first reaction is to beg you to try and try again. I truly believe with God all things are possible. But to you, these may just be pretty words that don't work. This doesn't make you a bad person. All I ask is you don't shut out the possibility that even if you can't do it today, this year or in the next decade, you will keep your mind open to the idea that one day it may be achievable.

Here is why it's so important. To work on forgiveness gives you power. It fills you with a sense of being bigger than your situation and certainly bigger than those who took so much from you. This empowers you to grow even stronger. It gives you roots in a firm belief system which will carry you through the hard times ahead. You will feel in closer harmony with God. If this is important to you, forgiveness is key. He does not ask us to do anything He doesn't do for us daily.

If you refuse to even consider forgiveness, while it's your choice, I don't believe you will experience an end point, or closure as it's so often called. There will always be a part of you that remains bitter. How can you truly grow into the kind of person you want to be with the unwillingness to forgive still festering deep in your soul?

I'll share a little secret with you. It has caused me terrible shame over the years. When I was about eight years old, I was molested by a deeply disturbed female babysitter. It's still hard for me to talk about. I had occasion to see her many years later when I attended my father's funeral. When I spotted her in the crowd I literally got nauseous and had to go outside.

Over the years I have been able to forgive a lot of people, eventually. The very thought of this ugly woman, however, still causes my stomach to turn. I am repulsed at the thought of her and the idea of forgiving her. As an ordinary human, I want her to burn forever for what she did. She disgusts me because she stole my innocence and distorted my view of myself. Yet, I force myself to flex my forgiveness muscle even for her. Why? Because if I don't she will always have that sickening effect over me and I won't allow it. Forgiving her means I can put her and all the loathsome memories attached to her in the ground and walk away.

One day I'll get there because I am determined. I continue to forgive (this, too is a process) her so I can have peace. It's my choice. But it's one I must make every time the memory of her floats into my head.

* * *

There is a saying that holding on to hate or unforgiveness is like drinking poison and waiting for the other person to die. This sums up my argument perfectly.

Forgiveness is a complicated and difficult topic. Only you can determine what is right for you. I pray you will choose to do

Vital Sign

Forgiveness is the last step in becoming whole.

By choosing not to forgive, you are the only

one who suffers.

it. In the end, it's the easier path – for you and you alone.

For example, when I look at my feeble mother who is dependent on my brother and me for everything, I simply can't be angry at her for those things of the past. It's ridiculous. I forgave her years ago. That doesn't mean she doesn't still push my buttons. The difference is now I am the adult, she is the child and I speak up. She has actually started saying, "I'm sorry," when she knows she's crossed the line; a first in my lifetime.

But there are days even now when I am overcome with anger at her. It ruins my whole day and the ironic part is because she has dementia, she forgets whatever it was she said that offended me five seconds later. Meanwhile, I'm still seething. So every day, I have to consciously forgive her and pray for more compassion. It's a never ending cycle, but it beats being lost in bitterness all the time. We will never be close in the way I had hoped for all my life and for that I still mourn occasionally. But this has nothing to do with forgiving her.

Forgiving my father did happen in a moment. It came as soon as I understood he was a sick man with many problems of his own which he never talked about. It was the easiest act of mercy I've experienced on my path to healing. Still, I'm sad I never really had a dad. But again, that is a separate thing entirely from forgiving him.

I still get angry at my ex-husband from time to time. Resentment can bubble up fast, instantly crowding forgiveness out of my thinking. The only difference is now I'm no longer a hostage to my thoughts. I make a conscious decision to stop the toxic thinking and do something else. When I remind myself he's not giving me a second thought, the obsession stops dead in its tracks. Now I can even smile at the silliness of it.

When I think of the guy I met in college so many years ago and what he did to me, I just feel pity for him now. It was easy for me to forgive him because that confused, scared girl he terrorized is gone and in her place is a wiser, stronger woman who sees how damaged he was along. It comes as no surprise to find out his father was an alcoholic and his childhood was filled with violence and dysfunction. As I said, it's generational.

> ## Vital Sign
> **Feeling sorrow or regret for what happened is not to be confused with forgiving or not forgiving.** *Sorrow is an emotion – a noun. Forgiveness is an action – a verb. A life of peace or one of constant angst hangs in the balance of that difference.*

What if the person you want to forgive for your own sake is still hurting you? The simple answer is what I said at the beginning of this truth: forgiveness is the last step in your healing process. If you are still involved with someone who is stealing your happiness and treating you badly, you aren't at the point of forgiving. You first have to work on developing boundaries, becoming self confident and making some tough decisions which will allow you get out of the relationship or at the very least, seriously change its dynamic before you can even consider forgiveness.

You must make your own peace of mind your focus. Leave the judgment to God. What others did to you is between them and Him. He gets to decide their fate, not you. Don't waste time obsessing over what they deserve. It's taken care of.

Forgiving yourself

There is no question here. You must make this a priority. If you can't forgive yourself, you are saying to God that what He has already done isn't good enough.

You will have to act as your own parent when you decide to get healthy. They were eager to punish and humiliate you or worse, gave you no direction whatsoever; but you are not them. Forgive yourself when you fall short, give a little mental pat on the back when you make progress and continue.

Remember, just like raising a toddler, forgiveness is a moment to moment affair. You are in fact, reconstructing your thinking, your behavior, your self-image and choices. Everything about you is being made new. You can only do this by making the occasional mistake. Forgive yourself and move on. Don't make a big thing over every misstep or momentary back-sliding that occurs. You're learning. Be patient with yourself. Learn to lighten up and laugh at yourself. It's wonderfully freeing. This is especially hard for the codependent personality, who is usually very serious and hard on himself. Just acknowledge it: "Boy am I acting like a codependent right now!" and keep going.

Being codependent, however, you will want to do it perfectly and obsess that someone is going to judge you. You will feel guilty that by taking this liberating action you may make another person uncomfortable. Your insecure, people-pleasing mania will kick in to the point of madness. Remind yourself this is your old way of thinking – do not allow the lie that you are not worthy of forgiveness run your life.

In conclusion, I love to quote my favorite spiritual teacher, the venerable Joyce Meyer. Sexually abused by her father for years, she took all the bad stuff that happened to her and turned it into a powerful message for good. She has gone on to become one of the best loved and most recognized Christian teachers in the world. I love her ability to combine down to earth common sense and humor to deliver spot-on messages.

One of her favorite stories is how it took Moses and the Israelites forty years to make a 12 day trip because they wouldn't listen to God. Her message is: 'How many times are you going to go around the same old mountain before you finally get it?"

This simple illustration has knocked sense into me on more than one occasion. So now I ask you, how many times are you going to let your past control you before you take charge by forgiving so you can get on with creating your good life?

Hanging on to the unwillingness to forgive – yourself or others – along with all the other negative emotions bundled up in that one decision, such as guilt, anger, shame, resentment, which cling like mold to your insides will only drain your precious energy. That same energy could be used right now for playing with your children, going for a walk, being creative, helping someone else or concentrating better so you could do your job in a more excellent way.

The decision to finally forgive is a huge one and not to be taken lightly. As I said earlier, there is much work to do before you can even get to the place where it's a possibility.

Once you truly believe you deserve to be free from the mental hold others have had over you, it will be time to consider your options. When you reach the point where you are strong enough to honestly say the ones who hurt you so badly have no power over you anymore, the decision to forgive won't be difficult. Only you will know when the time is right.

I wish you strength to give yourself the ultimate gift: freedom through forgiveness at the moment of your choosing.

PART THREE

A GUIDE TO RECOVERY THROUGH MINDFULNESS

"The past is gone, the future is not yet here, and if we do not go back to ourselves in the present moment, we cannot be in touch with life." – Thich Nhat Hanh

U p until now, we have exposed codependency for what it is, where it comes from and how it sabotages people's lives. To get here, you have been doing a lot of remembering and writing. This was no doubt hard because it takes time, which codependents never seem to have enough of, focus and honesty. It may have triggered painful emotions. Every time I sat down to work on this project, my heart would race at certain points. Feelings remain; changing the way I respond to those feelings has turned my life around.

Now the really hard work comes: Reclaiming your life. The reason the next step is so difficult is because it requires four commitments that do not come easily for people like us.

1. **Setting aside time to concentrate on your own well-being**. Codependents are not good at this. You will be fighting your own, non-stop reasoning mind which tells you

there isn't time (we are perpetually overwhelmed and short on time); you don't have the energy, you already know what to do, etc.

2. **Being willing to see yourself from a new perspective.** This is also very hard for codependent people. You have spent your whole life with a distorted concept of yourself, most of which is unhealthy and destructive.

3. **You must be ready to go from 'knowing' what to do in your head, to actually doing it.** Perhaps the hardest of all because all those old ways of thinking and automatic behaviors, while not productive, are natural to you in spite of their destructiveness. Nevertheless, you are going to have to do some things that absolutely go against the nature of the codependent such as not striving for *perfection*. There is no one right way or answer. You cannot let feelings of *guilt* run your thinking. In other words, everything that makes you codependent is going to be working against you here. Be aware of the paradox and persist.

4. **Most importantly, you have to believe you can be healed.** You must be able to see yourself as a fresh, new person with a healthy, balanced mind, body and lifestyle. Do you want this or not? Are you willing to stop making excuses, get past self-pity and guilt and do the real work of healing?

If you are really ready to change your life for the better, then this Guide will be a vital tool for you. It's not a magic formula; it's a lifestyle makeover. Nothing will go from miserable to wonderful over night. You are going to learn to use some new 'muscles.' None of this is a one-time exercise. In fact, you will find you're going to have to refer to this and other material often until you get your thinking changed.

Let's agree it's going to be hard but it is not only possible, it is essential in order for you to ever have a better life. You already have figured out you can't change anyone else, so you might as well do what you can: change yourself.

If you weren't hurting and desperate for help, you wouldn't be here right now. You are capable of doing what needs to be done if you stop trying to reason your way around the ideas I will lay before you and just do the work.

Codependent people are famous for chanting, "I know, I know," when others try to intercede and offer help. Having head knowledge is not the same as doing. Make a decision to let yourself be immersed in these ideas and practices, which may at first sound far-fetched, without judging and rationalizing. If you start to experience anxiety or feel distracted, walk away for a while. Return when you can focus.

Above all I need to stress again that what I offer is based in my own experience. The Guide is a compilation of information, beliefs and actions which over the years proved to be life altering for many people, including me.

CATEGORIES

Section I – Grieving the Past
Section II – Your Mind
Section III – Your Body
Section IV – Your Soul
Section V – Your Environment

SECTION ONE

GRIEVING THE PAST

"There are times when it becomes imperative to release a rage that shakes the skies...to let loose all the firepower one has."
– Clarissa Pinkola Estes, Ph.D.

Y ou have spent a lifetime erecting walls that protected you

and permitted you to function. The groundwork for these walls was laid in your past, most likely in your childhood. Awful hurdles such as addiction, abuse, trauma and endless shaming made it necessary for you to have protection from pain any way you could manage.

As I explained earlier, one very effective coping mechanism is to minimize those occurrences (they didn't mean it, it wasn't that bad, my brother had it much worse, etc.) Simply blocking them from your mind is also common. It's time to look at them honestly and go through them. Follow this simple process.

Step 1. – Face what happened in your past that set you up with all the wrong thinking you now live with. You wrote about it earlier. Go back, read what you wrote and take the time to really ponder all that information. Let it sink in. This requires you having the time and privacy to fully experience those memories.
Allowing yourself to grieve includes expressing your pent up

emotions. Codependents are experts at shoving their feelings so deep down they can't really feel anything. It's how we cope without falling to pieces every minute of the day. Now you are going to allow all those feelings to bubble up. If you need to lie down and think on purpose about your past, do it. Don't try to control your feelings, but do gently keep your thinking on track. You are beginning the process of mourning the death of many things including but not limited to your innocence, your childhood, your dreams, your individuality, your self esteem; whatever comes to your mind.

Step 2. Although it's not essential, keeping a journal just for this is very helpful. I found it's helpful to come back months and years later to read where I was at the beginning of my journey. Then I could see in black and white how far I had come in some areas and that I was still stuck in others. Remember, your healing will take a long time. It's good to have markers. It also helped me focus, since my mind is always going in a hundred directions.

- Who are you angry at?
- What did they do?
- Are they still doing it?
- How did their actions affect you? (Vital)

Step 3. Give yourself plenty of time here. Be aware of your breathing, your heart rate, your anxiety level. Notice if your thoughts are drifting. When this occurs, gently bring your thoughts back. Don't be critical of yourself. If you feel like you can't do this anymore, go to a different room or outside. When you feel calm again, go back. Review the events you were drawn to in your mind. If you want to write or draw something relating to your memories, do it. If you just want to be still and remember, that's good, too. Don't rush it. You are creating a starting place in your recovery by saying, in effect, "This happened to me. This is where my wrong thinking started. I had no choice. It was not my fault. I'm an adult now and I can change. This is where I have to begin." If you are inclined, pray for clarity and strength. Remember, don't concern yourself with forgiveness now. That's way down on your list of goals. Stay on task. Right now you are just exposing the sources of your pain. Again, I strongly encourage you to write or somehow put down your memories so you can add to and refer back to them later. Do what you need to in order to keep your mind focused. You need to be fully immersed in that time period. Notice what you're feeling and let it come out. This can take time and shouldn't be done when you have other tasks looming. It's also important to be alone, if possible. Note: If this is something you truly don't think you can handle doing by yourself, take the time to find a therapist who will work with you on past trauma.

Many codependents didn't have a pin-point moment or event which catapulted them into codependency. Rather it was the day to day dysfunction on some level that got their thinking screwed up. If this is the case with you, write about what the family dynamic was. Refer back to your notes in Part Two. Be very honest. It may be tempting to believe that because you weren't physically abused or traumatized in some way, that you have nothing to feel regret about. Were your parents so busy living 'the dream' they couldn't be bothered with the hassles of childrearing? Were you expected to be perfect to keep them looking just right? Did you feel loved only when you performed well or looked perfect? Look closer and connect the dots. Somewhere you were instilled with bad wiring. Where did it originate?

When you feel emotionally empty; stop. Be aware of the quiet around you and relax. Do you feel depleted, upset, fearful, angry, sad, numb or anxious? Make a mental note or write it down. All those feelings are normal. It would be odd if you didn't feel them. You may be highly emotional for a while. Or you may not. What matters is you uncovered those things which were kept in the dark up until now.

What you have done with this first step is simply to get honest with yourself and say, in effect, "These things happened. I have the right to be hurt, angry, etc." You are not going to stay here, though. It's just a first step. Identifying the source or the crossroad where your life got off track is very important. It means you are no longer in denial.

Everybody has a different story. You may need to get professional help working through all the emotions you experience when recalling these events. This is where a lot of people stop and there is no healing in obsessing about the past. It's just the first of many steps toward being set free.

Vital Sign

Acknowledging what happened is healthy.

Understanding you can't change what happened

or those involved is crucial.

Your goal is to change you, not them.

When you go back to your day, please don't go from 'resting' to 80 miles an hour. Ease into your routine. Give your brain a little time to switch back into routine mode.

Whenever a new thought or memory comes to you, write it down so you can focus on it later. You might as well get used to the idea of images popping into your head relating to your work here. There is a lot of uncovering and close examination to be done. Having a journal to refer to is so helpful. It represents a place where the pieces of your puzzle stay. You can add to it whenever it is appropriate. The puzzle will put itself together. Don't spend time reasoning and trying to figure it all out. Getting to the 'whys' will drive you crazy. It doesn't matter anymore. Simply observe your memories and feelings. Write them down. Notice how you are coping when they float into your head.

Remind yourself that what you're feeling regarding this exercise has nothing to do with what you are involved with during your normal day. Do not take out your sadness, anger, fear or panic on those around you. They are not part of this process.

You may have to go through these steps often before you're ready to move on. As long as you aren't obsessing, but rather adding on to what you can recall, keep at it.

Summary on grieving the past

- Remember, feel and record the events of your past

- You may need to go through this first step several times to retrieve all your memories and experience the emotions that are attached to them.

- Consider getting professional help to work through your emotional pain. This can be done with the help of a psychologist, a social worker, a counselor or the appropriate person at your church. Many of them have trained lay counselors whose services are usually free. Don't let money stop you. Most counselors and therapists are comfortable working on a sliding scale of payment, based on what you can pay. Also, if you have insurance be sure to check out your coverage. Most cover mental health in some way.

- Refrain from talking about this with friends and family. It's too easy to make it the topic of every conversation. That's obsessing and not healthy for you or them. Besides, it's private. Remember, everybody has stuff they are dealing with. Handle your own in the appropriate way and keep friends and family out of it. A well-meaning listener may inadvertently repeat something said in confidence which could have disastrous repercussions.

- Understand this is an ongoing effort, not a one-time project. Your mind has been filled with memories, lies and coping mechanisms all your life. It's going to take a long time to get all your information down and go through the natural emotions connected with them. Don't rush it.

- Don't get stuck in the remembering stage.

- If what you're grieving is still happening in a current relationship, you must put together a plan to get out of or modify it. If you are in danger, get out. If you are unhappy due to another person's choices, only you will know if by changing yourself you can find peace or if those choices are going to continue to be a hindrance to having the life you are working to have. If you truly believe the relationship is worth saving, both need to get counseling for whatever the problem is and commit to working things out.

- Resolving the past is not the goal. Learning not to let the past control you anymore is.

SECTION TWO

YOUR MIND

"There is only one perpetrator of evil on the planet: human unconsciousness." – Eckhart Tolle

I n the first section, you bravely allowed yourself to look back and see the wrong done to you. You were victimized, but to accept for the rest of your life that you are just a victim is to not be fully alive. It's also a lie. You are only a victim as long as you choose to be. Back then, you didn't have a choice. Now you do.

Although wrong thoughts were passed on to you which resulted in character traits and life choices you may now not be very happy with, you do have the option to change. You also have the responsibility to rectify those things about you which are negative and destructive. There comes a time when we have to stop blaming and start taking a deeper look at ourselves to correct our own wrong mindsets.

I've said it before and you've no doubt heard it many times: You can't change anybody but you. As much as you would like to make that other person straighten up, you can't. As you already know, trying day in and day out to fix other people is a whole lot easier than taking a close look at your own faults and working on them. That's precisely why codependents are their own worst enemy.

Today, you are going to look in the mirror of your mind and take an inventory of those things you know are holding you back. There's a reason why the 12 Step Program is based on this concept.

Yes, people did terrible things to and around you. But now you're an adult. It's time to do the work of becoming a better person in spite of your past. Let's start at the beginning. Do you really know who you are, what makes you tick and where you need help? Codependent people struggle with many issues including:

Controlling behavior
Manipulation
Insecurity
Anger
Easily offended
Anxiety
Depression
Fearful of rejection
Trouble making decisions
Distorted thinking
Overly responsible followed by being irresponsible
Numb – out of touch with feelings
Highly emotional or completely out of touch with their feelings
Constant guilt
Overly apologetic
Trouble focusing
Consumed with other people's lives/needs
Drawn to same types of dysfunctional people repeatedly
Obsessed with looking and acting perfect
Poor or non-existent boundaries
Easily frustrated

Care-taker personality
Defensive
Trouble with intimacy
Self-neglect/abuse
Tendency toward addiction or addictive activities
Overly serious (difficulty playing, laughing, or being silly)
Overly dramatic
Filled with regrets
Lie easily
Tendency to quit before completing things
Feel out of control often
Reason and rationalize too much

Add any other traits you believe are keeping you stuck.

_____

_____

_____

Everybody has some of these problems some of the time. Codependents have most of them most of the time. That's why it's vital to understand how it's affecting your life.

Now, write down the five biggest issues out of all of these which are keeping you from being whole and happy. Then write down what the opposite would be.

Example: **Need to control**   **Supportive but not involved**

_____   _____

_____   _____

_____   _____

_____   _____

_____   _____

Write down how you believe these negative traits are affecting you and those around you. What has it cost you?

_____

_____

_____

_____

_____

This provides you with a starting place to focus on those traits deserving attention first in order for you to move forward.

The way to recover from everything on this list and anything else keeping you stuck can be boiled down to one word. It is the solution for any problematic personality traits you may suffer with. The word is: MINDFULNESS

Mindfulness

It's a simple word and not revolutionary or magical. It has come into the mainstream recently thanks to the scientific work of such notable scholars as John Kabit-Zinn, PhD, Herbert Benson, M.D., Buddhist monk, Thich Nhat Hanh and other practitioners in the field of mental well-being around the world. A practical definition of mindfulness, according to Kabit-Zinn is: *"A way of self-transformation through self-observation."* This is practiced without judgment or condemnation; hard for the codependent to do. We love to beat ourselves up for not doing things perfectly.

The simple truth is that becoming aware of how you feel, think, talk, respond to others and your own thoughts is a proven way to retrain yourself over a period of time to think and behave differently.

It's is similar to Cognitive Behavioral Therapy (CBT) which asserts that 'Our thoughts cause our feelings and behaviors, not external things such as people, events and situation. We can change the way we think in order to feel and act better even if the situation doesn't change.' [4] The huge difference is that mindfulness isn't just about being aware of how we think. It also asks us to notice – in a non-condemning way – how we respond to others, how we act, speak and function in the world. In other words, it is a multi-dimensional observation.

Every item on the list at the beginning of this section is really just a bad habit. They are flawed coping mechanisms born out of a need to either protect or as a way of behaving to get the one illusive thing the codependent so craves: acceptance.

Control, perfectionism, rigidity, people-pleasing.....every single one of them is just a faulty way of helping you function in the world because you were not instilled with right thinking at the time when you should have been taught the skills to be a healthy individual. Instead, you were caught up in dysfunctional parenting, possibly addiction, abuse, shame, trauma and too much stress for a child to properly assimilate.

In short, all these negative attributes stem from a deeply troubled start in life. They are second nature to you. It may feel like there is no way you could ever *not* be these things. That is the mindset of codependency. But this too, is a lie.

Ironically, one of the things codependent people do best is to be continually hyper-vigilant to their surroundings like wild animals; always listening and watching lest they be attacked. Yet, for all their awareness, they are blind when it comes to seeing how inappropriate, negative or incongruent their behavior is. In Part Two when I wrote about the lie **"I'm crazy"**, I described Distorted Thinking. Go back and reread what it means. You will see how important it is to understand most of what you're

---

[4]   National Association of Cognitive Behavioral Therapists.

thinking is automatic and negative in nature rather than intentional and healthy.

The missing link is mindfulness. Not the kind where we obsess about our shortcomings and beat ourselves up all day long which is another habit born out of defective thinking, but the kind of gentle awareness which gradually reinforces new, healthier ways to think, feel and behave.

Kabit-Zinn, adds that mindfulness is "Self reflection – not obsessing." Of course obsessing is what codependents are really good at. Watching without judgment – just being – is like asking for the impossible.

Mindfulness asks us not to control what happens. But we crave the control! Instead, the goal is just to notice. Change will come when we see over and over again that a healthier way of thinking, speaking or behaving brings a new and better response. Mindfulness allows us to look at ourselves with kindness and self-compassion. This goes against our powerful self-loathing and constant negative self-talk.

Mindfulness opens our mind to see the good within us. We aren't comfortable with that; instead we love to pick at our weaknesses like open, painful sores.

Remember, as I explained early on, the paradox for the codependent is that the very things which define you are the same things you will have to overcome in order to become who you want to be. In essence you are your own worst enemy. But every enemy has a weak spot. If, as the quote by Eckhart Tolle at the beginning of this section suggests, the only evil in the world is human unconsciousness, then the opposite would be mindfulness.

In Part One, I explained the Hierarchy of Enlightenment. Mindfulness fits right into this process. Kabat-Zinn sums up the parallel: *"It's not what you know, it's what you're willing to know you don't know"* which is revealed in mindfulness. Rather than being busy with fixing ourselves, he simply asks us to observe.

This is a hard one for us.

Asking a codependent person to be quiet just for a moment and go inward is like asking a shark to stop swimming - it's what we think we must do or we will be overcome with painful feelings, thoughts and memories. But it can be done. Only when you reach your personal breaking point and are sick and tired of being a negative, ineffective person who is always getting the same bad results in life – can you truly change. I can say this because I've been there. You can be mindful in your daily life by just being aware of yourself in a compassionate manner.

For example:

- I notice I am feeling anxious again.

- I mentally step back and observe my thoughts and physical sensations without beating myself up.

- I realize I'm obsessing about an encounter I had with someone a day earlier. Over and over I play it out in my mind, getting worked up all over again. I notice I am no longer tuned into what is going on around me, but lost in my harmful thoughts.

- I take a deep breath and tell myself (out loud if I'm alone) that my reaction is just a bad habit. I deliberately stop the negative thinking, which brings me back into the moment.

- I focus on my breathing and realize it's rapid and shallow. I consciously take some deep, cleansing breaths.

- I purposefully change what I choose to think about; I pay

attention to what is actually happening around me, rather than in my head.

- I focus on what is real (my anxious ruminations are lies). "I am ok right now. The situation I'm feeling anxious about does not have control over me."

- I continue to breathe deeply and purposefully and I feel my heart slowing down; my body relaxing.

- I am easy on myself. I know at first this will probably not make much difference, but in time, I understand I will have retrained the way I think -and therefore feel- about situations I tend to obsess about or feel stressed over.

This may sound trite and ineffective now. But I promise if you dare to commit to it, small changes will eventually begin happening in your thinking. This is because you are no longer operating out habitual, stale reflexes. You are becoming aware – in a healthy way – about how you interact with others in your day to day world. You are developing awareness about what you are thinking, how you are breathing, your tension level and your response to outside triggers. You will soon discover you do have control over yourself. You can be deliberate in your responses to situations and events. In the above example (which is a true experience), I had to continually say to myself in lighthearted manner, "There you go again," with an inner smile. It was my way of jostling my thoughts. Then I would go on to the next step.
Typical responses to the idea of turning your thinking around are, "My whole family is like that, I can't help it." *Yes you can.* "That's just my personality, I can't change that." *Yes you can.*

Although this concept wasn't widely popular back when I

realized I had to change the way I thought and behaved if I was ever going to improve my life, I was still doing exactly what has now been proved as scientifically effective for things like depression, anxiety, other wrong mindsets and even physical pain. I wish all this help had been around back then, but the fact it wasn't is further proof that if you really want to grow, you can, using whatever resources are available.

Take one of the top five traits you're concerned with and use it to do this exercise

• I am feeling (or doing)_____again.

• Notice your thoughts, how your body is reacting (twitches, pain, muscle tightness).

• Pay attention to your breathing. Is it shallow or rapid? Purposefully breathe slow and deep. Notice your heartbeat. Slow, intentional breaths will make your heart slow down.

• Consciously feed yourself positive, true messages: "I don't have to feel _____(guilty, scared, angry, regretful, controlling, needy, etc). These are old habits. I do not have to believe the old reasons for my behavior anymore. I am in charge of my feelings. If I need to say 'no' to someone in order to feel better today, I can do it. I am safe. I am loved by God. I am forgiven. I can change this." Don't worry about if these words 'take' or not. Just quietly say them.

• Purposefully return to what is happening around you, rather than being in your head. When your mind wanders back to painful thoughts or you feel negative physical sensations coming on again, gently repeat those positive words to yourself.

* Notice your breathing again; your heart rate; your thoughts. Be aware that you are not feeling out of control, instead you feel more grounded and calmer.

If you find yourself judging how well you're doing and being critical, remember to be easy on yourself. Acknowledge this is a new muscle you have found and it's going to take time to make it strong. You are being mindful. Over time, every thinking and emotional problem you are struggling with can be minimized and eventually neutralized by your new awareness.

When you are in a situation with someone and you find yourself about to react in an old, negative way, take one deep breath - this allows you to step back and observe the situation, then make a decision about how you choose to respond. This is the one extra second that will change how you live your life. Most people don't use it. They just automatically think, respond, feel, talk, react; all with the same problematic outcomes. **By giving yourself this one extra second, you are going from unconscious to mindful.**

Will you shout, be defensive, controlling, negative, fearful, intimidated, angry, phony (saying 'yes' when you mean 'no', smiling when you are really angry); or will you choose to see yourself as a new person and respond with calmness and a noticeable lack of all the old traits? By being aware – mindful – of yourself and your situation, you have a choice. Over time the choice will become easier until one day it will become a new, healthy habit.

Breathing as a tool for mindfulness
*"Feelings come and go like clouds in a windy sky.
Conscious breathing is my anchor."*
– Thich Nhat Hanh

When I was feeling especially tense, I had a habit of not breathing. I would just stop breathing as my mind would obsess and worry. This brought on sensations of near panic. Then I would have to tell myself to breathe. It sounds ridiculous, but it's true.

The way we breathe has a profound effect on how we function, I've since learned. Rapid, shallow breathing keeps our bodies feeling like we are in crisis. Full, deep intentional breaths bring calm and a sense of being well grounded.

One of the key aspects of being mindful is to become aware of our breathing and then to breathe in such a way as to slow our heart down and allow our brains to properly assimilate what is going on both within and around us.

There are hundreds of books, DVD's and CD's explaining the benefits of proper breathing. One of the most easy to understand and concise explanations in my opinion, is an important book I've already made reference to, *A New Earth, Awakening to Your Life's Purpose* by Eckhart Tolle. Because his writing about breathing is so clear and succinct, I am including it for your benefit. Information on his book and website are in the Resource section.

"Another simple but highly effective way of finding space in your life is closely linked to the breath. You will find that by feeling the subtle flow of air in and out of the body as well as the rise and fall of your chest and abdomen, you are also becoming aware of the inner body. Your attention may then shift from the breath to that felt aliveness within you, diffuse throughout the body.

Most people are so distracted by their thoughts, so

identified with the voices in their heads; they can no longer feel the aliveness within them (italics added). To be unable to feel the life that animates the physical body, the very life that you are, is the greatest deprivation that can happen to you. You then begin to look not only for substitutes for that natural state of well-being within, but also for something to cover up the continuous unease that you feel when you are not in touch with the aliveness that is always there but usually over-looked. Some of the substitutes people seek out are drug-induced highs, sensory over stimulation such as excessively loud music, thrills or dangerous activities, or an obsession with sex. Even drama in relationships is used as a substitute for that genuine sense of aliveness (*another great description of codependency – JM*). The most sought after cover-up for the continuous background unease are intimate relationships; a man or a woman who is going to "make me happy." It is, of course, also one of the most frequently experienced of all the "letdowns." And when the unease surfaces again, people will usually blame their partner for it.

Take two or three conscious breaths. Now see if you can detect a subtle sense of aliveness that pervades your entire inner body. Can you feel your body from within, so to speak? Sense briefly specific parts of your body. Feel your hands, then your arms, feet and legs. Can you feel your abdomen, chest, neck and head? What about your lips? Is there life in them? Then become aware again of the inner body as a whole. You may want to close your eyes initially for this practice and once you can feel your body, open your eyes, look around and continue to feel your body at the same time."

Codependents are notorious for not only being out of touch with their emotions, but their bodies as well. Tolle's point regarding breathing in this context is to use breathing to get in touch with the inner self. It is a personal 'time out' in which we go inward and reconnect with our own body so we can then connect with others.

Take a breath

Different ways of breathing bring different results. To relax, I've learned that putting my hand on my abdomen (the area around my belly button) helped. When breathing in through the nose, force the abdomen to extend outward. Take in a comfortable, deep breath. Feel you entire rib cage and torso expand. Hold it a second. Then, exhale, ideally through the mouth, but nose is okay, while pulling the abdomen muscles in. Exhale completely. Usually, if you try, you will find there is a little air left to be pushed out.

Normally, we inhale from the chest. The shoulders go up and we suck our tummies in. That is not intentional breathing, it's habit. When we get nervous our breathing gets shallow or as was my habit, stops all together until we panic.

By putting your hand on your abdomen as you breathe, be aware that you are now taking air in through your diaphragm; this is good. This will also have the added benefit of working out your abdominal muscles, making them more taut. Once you get the hang of abdominal breathing, you won't need to put your hand there. You don't have to assume any special position to breathe this way, although I've found when I'm really stressed, laying down helps. Whenever you sense you're not getting enough air or feel anxious, put your attention on your abdomen and just breathe. Remember, as I said at the very beginning of this book, you have to participate in your own healing. Learning and doing are essential.

Challenges requiring mindfulness

The list of things we need to become mindful of in order to begin the process of changing is – as we saw previously – a long one. The issues are different, but the answer is the same. We must become aware of how we are thinking and responding in order to intentionally change those traits which are keeping us from having peace. I've pulled out a few that are common for the codependent which were (and sometimes still are) areas I had to walk the walk before I could talk the talk by writing this book.

Control and perfectionism – One of the hardest things for a codependent person to do is to stop trying to control everybody and everything in their world. The reason we devote our lives to it is because of a lie we were fed long ago: **I am not good enough**. So if I can make everything around me perfect then maybe the person I needed approval from way back then will finally love me. Maybe the whole world will not look at me and see a fraud and a failure. If I make everything just right, no one will notice how unlovable I really am. These are such damaging beliefs. Here are some useful tools I picked up over the years that helped me release the grip control and perfectionism had on me.

- Notice how exhausting and futile it is to feel in charge of the universe.

- Get comfortable with silence. Stop filling it with endless advice, opinions, suggestions, gossip, rearranging, interfering, etc.

- Learn to take a breath (mindfulness), smile and encourage the other person to make their own decisions.

- Be supportive but not involved. Get accustomed to not being right or in charge constantly.

- Incorporate simple phrases like, "Oh well," or "It's not my job to fix that," into your lexicon. It sounds silly, but it is incredibly freeing because it takes you off the hook in other people's eyes, and it feeds your brain new beliefs which are healthier.

- Remember the example you are setting for your kids and other loved ones. The more controlling you are with and around them, the more you push them away.

- As a daily exercise, notice one little thing you feel the need to make perfect and make the decision to let it be. It will drive you nuts at first, but eventually, you'll start enjoying being more carefree.

Anger – You have a multitude of things to be angry about, but to let anger be your identity is not healthy and not how you were meant to live.

- If you're angry at someone in particular, work toward being able to talk to that person, discuss the problem and work it out. If that isn't an option (person is dead, lives far away, is dangerous) then talk to a professional to work through your feelings.

- Scream into a pillow or pound on it to blow steam. Do it privately. This may sound simplistic, but trust me, it works.

- Walk, run, ride a bike or do some sort of physical workout to help get rid of the excess emotion.

- If you are angry because people are taking advantage of you, See upcoming section on Boundaries (page 126). Learning to speak up *effectively* is an invaluable tool for relieving anger.

- If forgiveness is in the equation of your process in working through anger, read **Truth #5** again and put together your plan.

- Refrain from chemicals that cause mood swings such as caffeine, sugar, alcohol. Rising and falling blood sugar can trigger feelings ranging from irritability to rage.

- When your thinking turns toward anger and negativity, utilize the mindfulness exercises and breathe.

"We only hate when we feel totally powerless." Alice Miller, PhD.

Depression – As a therapist once told me, depression is anger turned inward. If you're still holding on to anger, you won't be able to overcome the debilitating effects of depression.

- Deal with your anger (re-read previous page)

- You need to have an ongoing relationship with a therapist or counselor you trust and can be honest with.

- Educating yourself is always a must. Read everything you can on what causes depression (this goes for every disorder or problem you're dealing with). It is very possible that in addition to circumstances that are keeping you down, you may have some physical problems which are causing depression-like symptoms. In the next section on the body, we'll get into more detail.

- Write! You don't have to be a writer to put your thoughts down on paper. By looking at what you're thinking about and making note of how you feel both mentally and physically, you will be able to see your progress. You will also be surprised to see what comes through you. Things you have suppressed or forgotten may emerge.

- Find a support group. Depressed people like to isolate. This is the worst thing you can do. Everybody needs a day alone now and then, but when you start avoiding everybody because you are just too depressed, you must force yourself to be with others who understand. Get to the source of your depression, and then find an appropriate support group to help you work through it. A list of national support groups is in the Resource section. Warning! Remember, it can become easy to slip into the mindset that your 'issues' are your life. Don't get into this rut. Support groups are important but not meant to be your entire existence.

- Be open to taking medication. In Part Two, I discussed the different types of depression. Sometime medication helps tremendously even if you only use them for a while. Most take about 4-6 weeks to show signs of helping, so be patient. Find a good doctor, get a physical to make sure there aren't any other problems and talk about your depression. There are many good medications to choose from these days. While some people use them for a period of time, others stay on them a lifetime. It's a personal decision. In most cases, they are not the solution, merely a band-aid to 'stop the bleeding' so you can begin working on the source of your issues. With others, a medical condition is causing depression and medication will alleviate much of the problem.

- Do not indulge in endless talk about your problems to anybody who will listen. It's usually not productive and only keeps your thoughts stuck.

- Train your brain (mindfulness) not to obsess. This is an easy trap for a depressed person to fall into.

- Stop the 'magical thinking'. "If only he would just die then I would be happy." "If only......."

- Be aware of yourself (mindfulness) when you are numbing yourself with things like work, busy-ness, drugs, alcohol, television, food, sleeping. These are all forms of denial and will only make you feel more guilty.

- This is another problem that is increased by the use of chemicals such as caffeine, alcohol, drugs, too much sugar, etc. Anything that influences your mood can intensify depression. Be mindful of what you put in your system and how it affects you.

Guilt – Nobody does guilt like a codependent. We wake up feeling guilty before we even know why. It's a habit and it's destructive. Pervasive guilt is part of the DNA for us, but once the source is discovered, the process of disengaging from it becomes doable over time.

- Remind yourself that you are an adult and not a child seeking approval which will never come. This is especially true for the people who were given the message they were loved not for who they were, but for what they did. But the doing is never enough, thus guilt is ever present.

- Take an inventory. Is your guilt justified? Do you need to make something right? Find the right time and place and do it. It could be as simple as saying, "I'm sorry." Then purposefully, intentionally let it go. If you can't make it right because the person is gone or there are other circumstances preventing it, pray for forgiveness, receive it and teach yourself to stop feeling guilt over it. This is another habit that needs to be turned around. It will take time. Be patient.

- Ask yourself if you are carrying someone else's guilt. Were you raised, for example, by an insecure parent who passed his or her guilt on to you leaving you feeling as if something was wrong with you which warranted ongoing guilt? The close examination of your past which you did earlier in the book will help with this.

- Instead of beating yourself up every day for an endless list of guilt-driven reasons, try doing small, nice things for yourself. And don't let guilt seep in and ruin it.

- Ask yourself if you would make anybody else feel this lousy and guilty all the time. Of course not.

- Learn to say 'no'. Then allow yourself to enjoy it.

- Guilt is very often a lingering effect of lies you believed in the past about who you were. You believed the lies discussed in Part Two and many more. Noticing that "I'm feeling guilty again and I don't even know why!" is proof your feeling is an old habit. Habits can be changed with practice.

Boundaries – When healthy boundaries are not formed in our early years, we don't have a good sense of who we are. In dysfunctional families, it's often hard to know where one person leaves off and the other begins. For example, a child of a chemically dependent parent might feel responsible for keeping the adult happy because if she doesn't there could be an ugly consequence. At an early age, children in homes where there is addiction, abuse or mental instability learn to be overly responsible. In doing so, they lose their ability to be playful and spontaneous as adults. They also fear saying 'no' because they might suffer. This is especially true where sexual abuse is present.

People with poor boundaries:

- Say 'yes' when they want to say 'no' or 'no' when they mean 'yes'
- Suffer from depression, low energy, identity loss, eating disorders and other addictive habits, low self esteem and feel over whelmed constantly
- Struggle with intimacy (i.e. have sex when they don't want to, feel resentful and angry, can't perform, agree to do things they don't want to, can't develop genuine closeness)
- Tend to be either overly responsible or very irresponsible
- Have panic attacks and often feel 'out of control'
- May be terrified of being alone and are very needy
- Have difficulty making and keeping healthy friendships
- Feel like victims, are resentful and have passive-aggressive tendencies
- Have pervasive, ongoing guilt and anxiety

It's exhausting when you not only have to control the world and feel responsible for everybody's happiness, all while feeling completely overwhelmed and resentful because the people you are trying to help are taking advantage of you. To make matters worse, it's never enough, so you have guilt. It is no wonder codependent people struggle with depression and addiction. Life feels unbearable much of the time.

To help you put some boundaries in your life, here are a few ideas given to me which I still use.

- Remind yourself you are an adult, not a needy child seeking approval from everybody because you never got it as a child.

- Be aware (mindful) of the way you carry yourself and respond to people; right down to the tone of your voice. I realized years ago that when I was uncomfortable or intimidated, my voice actually sounded like a little girl's. I had to train myself to talk like a grown up. Your behavior should reflect the fact that you see yourself as a stable adult.

- While you are not above anyone else (sometimes we over compensate for our insecurities by acting haughty) you are not below them, either. You are equal.

- Take the plunge and say 'no' to someone's request to take on a new responsibility. Do not apologize. Be kind. Thank them for the opportunity and simply say you can't take on anything else right now and leave it at that. Well-adjusted people will accept it with graciousness. Manipulators will be put off. You will quickly discover which ones you're dealing with. It will be much easier to say 'no' the next time a manipulator tries to corner you.

- After each time you have successfully responded honestly to another person – either saying 'yes' when you meant it (Yes, I'd love some help.) or 'no' (No, I'm sorry, I can't join you Saturday morning. Thanks for asking.) Reward yourself. Try a special cup of coffee (decaf!), a little gift, etc.

- Set aside time each week – even if it is just a half hour – to be alone. It doesn't matter what you're doing. The point is you are learning to be comfortable being with yourself. You don't need people showering you with attention all the time and offering constant validation to feel human. Be aware of how your heart pounds and your thoughts race at first (mindfulness). Accept this is happening and it's normal. Discipline yourself to be alone for the time you've allotted. And don't spend it on Facebook, texting or calling people!

- Incorporate reading, praying, writing, drawing, even meditating - remember meditating is worrying in reverse-into your daily routine. Pay attention to how you are changing and getting stronger.

- When you feel impulsivity moving in, make a conscious decision to rethink it. Look ahead at how you are going to feel after you've indulged again. Be aware (mindful) that you are breaking another form of habitual behavior. When you successfully refuse to be impulsive, reward yourself in a healthy way. Note it in your journal.

- Write about your experience. Are your depression, anxiety, low energy, panic attacks better or worse when you draw a line in the sand and stand up for yourself? Do you feel more in charge of your emotions?

- Accept the fact that by saying 'no' to certain people, they will abandon you. You won't die. You needed to let them go. You will be lonely for a while, but you need this time to grow. In time people who are more in line with the healthier person you are becoming will surface and you will enjoy authentic relationships, rather than 'one up, one down' scenarios.

- Allow yourself to speak up. You have been trained by the lies of your past to keep your mouth shut because if you said the wrong thing, punishment or worse – rejection - would be forthcoming. It's frightening at first and feels unnatural to disagree or to have a differing opinion. Become mindful of the fact that you are just as entitled to an opinion as the other person. As your boundaries become stronger, you will notice you can speak up more easily over time. Notice people don't hate you for it and the world doesn't stop spinning. What you are doing in an appropriate, kind manner is what normal, well-adjusted people do every day.

Addiction: It's not unusual for a person who is living with or was raised with a chemically dependent person to have this tendency. Also, a many people choose addiction as a way of coping with the drama that is codependency. Cigarettes, alcohol, drugs, sex, food – even chronic laziness can all lead to their own sets of consequences. Habitual bad habits used to numb out feelings can lead to devastating results. Addiction is a common denominator in many codependents' lives. Maybe you were raised with it and now it's got a hold on you. That's why I talked about it extensively at the beginning of this book. It is a huge problem and a separate subject all of its own. Many books and other sources of information are available for those struggling with it and I have included the main ones in the Resource section. If this is an area of concern for you, it's imperative that you start at the beginning and acknowledge you have a problem. To invest in being physically healthy as a step in overcoming codependency, you must first get clean. This too, begins with being mindful. Once you are at a point in your recovery where you can see who you really are and what pushed you toward addiction, chances are your next challenge will be to overcome codependency. My belief is if you have beat addiction, you can certainly beat this. People who choose sobriety each day are some of the strongest individuals I know.

Anything you need to work on can be worked through by utilizing mindfulness. My hope is that you will give it a chance to help you become the truly alive and peaceful person you were always meant to be.

* * *

To close this section on the mind, I think it's important to talk a little about the positives. You have a lot of them. Books of this nature focus on the problems, which makes it easy to forget that in spite of whatever mess you're in at this moment, you have plenty of wonderful qualities.

Those things which make you codependent also make you a special type of person. I've had many years to reflect on my shortcomings. Finally, when I wasn't beating myself into a bloody pulp every day, I began to allow the idea that just maybe I was lovable after all to sink in.

It feels uncomfortable at first. For every good thing I thought about myself, there was a little voice in my head saying the opposite. Nevertheless, at least I was seeing these things for the first time. It felt good. For example:

If you are controlling, you are probably also very caring

and dependable. If you are hurting, you are no doubt attuned to the fact that others around you hurt, too. If you are a fixer, caretaker or rescuer, you are also a giver. If you are overwhelmed and exhausted, it's probably because in your heart you are doing your very best to help the ones you care about. Your motives are good even if they are not ultimately healthy for you.

You are a good person doing the best you know how. That's admirable.

Summary on the mind

- Take an honest look at those traits which are holding you back in life.
- Practice being Mindful to undo any negative thoughts and behaviors.
- Incorporate relaxation breathing into your daily routine.
- Be patient with yourself as you gradually learn new ways to function.
- You have positive qualities. Accept that you are a good person.

SECTION THREE

YOUR BODY

"In order to change we must be sick and tired of being sick and tired." – Unknown

I n the section about **Truth #3**, I touched on the physical

consequences of codependency. By its very nature, it sets a person up for physical problems. Addiction, depression, lethargy, self-neglect, and stress are few of the outcomes of this disorder which over time can ravage the body. If you haven't taken care of yourself, or if you have physical issues that are consuming your energy, you can't possibly have the focus or the stamina to work on things of the mind. You're too distracted by fatigue, pain, immobility, etc.

At the beginning of this Guide, I asked you to set aside time for your own healing and to be willing to see yourself from a new perspective. Part of this newness is having a healthy body. I discovered that if I didn't move due to depression or flat out exhaustion, I got more depressed until I couldn't do anything. It was a horrible, vicious cycle; one that ate up huge chunks of time. It took me years to figure out and accept that my periods of deep depression ran directly parallel to times I did not do some sort of regular exercise. My biggest obstacle – depression - turned into my greatest motivator. By years of painful experience, I learned the steep price I would pay if I stopped working out.

Additionally, ongoing stress burns us out. The "Fight or Flight" response we all have gets abused until we suffer adrenal burnout, which I also experienced. After a lifetime of being on my guard, living in fear, over-working, over-thinking, over-worrying and in general being a nervous wreck because I was trying to control and perfect everything, it took next to nothing to upset me or wear me out. I was sick constantly and always tired. I cried easily, was jumpy and exhausted.

Just before I literally crashed, I couldn't concentrate. My patience and memory were getting worse. Everything I tried to do went wrong and I felt like a complete failure which brought on more guilt. I had no choice but to get off the 'hamster wheel' and do the bare minimum to start feeling normal. It took two years. My adrenal glands were shot from pumping adrenalin 24/7 my whole life. Not only was it unhealthy but left unchecked, it could have led to more serious issues.

The fact that your physical health and your mental well-being are intricately connected is inescapable. You can't let your body go to pot and hope to feel good. It's just not going to happen. I'm not asking you to become an athlete (we have that all or nothing mentality, I know) but taking care of your body is a vital part of your healing. It's time to take a closer, honest look how healthy you are.

Step one - your physical inventory

Start by making a list of any physical issues you have or have had off and on throughout your life. Include any bad habits or addictions you have. Jot down next to them any diagnosis and treatments you've had. Refer to Part One where you wrote down some related information.

1._____

2._____

3._____

If you need more room, use your journal (which I hope you've been keeping!)

Write down a number, on a scale from one to ten indicating how healthy you feel right now. _____

From here, you will begin another new chapter in your life. You have committed to getting well in all ways within your control. It'll be interesting to refer back to this a year from now and see how far you've come.

I'm willing to go out on a limb and say most of the symptoms you are dealing with were created out of ongoing stress and disharmony in your body and mind. This is precisely why the Holistic Health movement gained so much momentum once it hit the mainstream. Its basis lies in the belief that the body, mind and soul are connected. When one is out of whack, the others will suffer also. If your back hurts, your energy level drops, your thinking slows down and soon you may start to feel depressed because you can't do those things you need or want to. Your faith in yourself wanes. On the flip side, if you are struggling with depression, you won't want to exercise or eat right so your body becomes sluggish, making you feel even more hopeless. It's a system that is interwoven. To deny the health of one is to endanger all three.

Codependency confines us to our heads too much. We spend a lot of time worrying, obsessing, trying to reason, rationalize, get lost in distorted or magical thinking and often times we put our physical health on the back burner.

The other culprit is self-loathing. If you hate yourself because you've bought into the lies listed in Part Two, or if you've lived in such a way that you are filled with guilt, shame and remorse, you could easily fall into punishing yourself by indulging in dangerous habits, addictions and a generally sloppy

144

lifestyle. This is another outcome of codependency.

Then there are the defining characteristics of the codependent which over time are guaranteed to wear our bodies down: lack of boundaries, doing too much, feeling overwhelmed, exhaustion and on top of all that, we keep going because we truly believe we have no choice. Add the side effects of various possible addictions (smoking, alcoholism, drug abuse, over eating, etc.) and you may be functioning at the bare minimum.

Let's take a closer look at the main bad habits that affect you in the physical realm. Then go back, look at those top health issues you're struggling with and see what behaviors need to change in order to reclaim your vitality.

Stress

A life without some stress would be boring. Everybody has stress and to some degree that's a good thing. Normal stress isn't the problem for codependent people. We live with a toxic stress which was set in motion and became as natural to us as breathing long ago. Tumultuous homes and relationships, unnatural degrees of chaos, violence, fear and tension are common for the person raised in dysfunctional families. This creates the kind of stress that never really goes away. I talked about the Fight or Flight syndrome. Many people suffer with it. When you don't feel safe you will be on your guard. When you are constantly being vigilant, you will be stressed. This way of living eventually turns into just another bad habit born out of what seems like a necessity at the time.

Stress run rampant has many negative effects on the body:

- High blood pressure
- The nervous system is perpetually stimulated to unhealthy degrees
- The body holds on to belly fat (cortisol imbalance)

- Digestive system develops problems: indigestion, ulcers, irritable bowel, acid reflux, constipation, colitis
- Premature aging
- Clouded thinking and memory problems
- Sleep disturbances
- Interference with proper insulin levels
- Tendencies toward addiction to calm down
- Fatigue
- Short temper, anger and depression
- Poor eating habits
- Lack of exercise or extreme workouts that deplete the body even more

As if all that wasn't enough, there is growing proof that ongoing stress, if not dealt with, has been linked to diseases such as cancer because the immune system becomes compromised.

Stress alone is reason enough to be willing to whatever it takes to turn your thinking around.

Reducing stress

- **Delegate** – this is one of the hardest things a controller can do. We have this crazy idea that nobody else could possibly do it right. We are indispensable. But we are wrong. Learning to delegate is essential if there is to be a lessening of stress levels. One of the main reasons delegating is nearly impossible for people is it's so hard to speak up and ask. Think of this as just another muscle you must get in shape if you're going to have a less stressed out life. If you ask nicely, without apologizing which we are notorious for doing, most people are happy to help. Remember, other people want to feel needed, too. Especially our children.

- **Ask yourself 'why'** – Why do you hang on to so many commitments? Is it because you're afraid you'll be replaced or forgotten? Are you terrified of letting someone down or losing their affection? Do you not know your own limits since you haven't been paying attention to the signs your body is giving you as in the previous list? Honest reflection on this question will reveal what you are really looking for. Do you honestly believe you're the only one who has enough sense to get everything done right? If so, you're teaching those around you to be helpless and users.

- **Say "No"** - Once you learn how to say 'no' as talked about in the Mindfulness section, you will be able to trim the excess responsibility from your schedule. I guarantee it will feel scary at first, like walking off a plank blindfolded because you are so afraid of rejection. But in reality, normal people say 'no' all the time and don't think a thing about it. People accept it, too, without being dramatic. It's an adult way of conducting yourself and the best part is others will respect you more and you will feel good about yourself.

  I got tired of taking on one project after another that I really didn't want to, losing interest half way through, resenting everybody for 'talking me into it' and eventually either dropping the ball or doing a half-baked job, both of which only added to my ongoing guilt. Saying 'no' is much easier. Again, if done with kindness and grace, saying 'no' will have the right results.

- **Say "Yes"** – With all our focus on the importance of learning how to say 'no', I don't want to leave out the very important matter of learning how to say 'yes' at the right times. As controllers, we think we can do it all. If others offer to help, train yourself to accept it. Saying 'yes' is an important part of giving up control. And it empowers others, including family members.

- **Move!** – The tendency to collapse on the couch with a block of cheese and a bottle of wine is tempting when we feel stressed out. Exercising is not on the radar when we are exhausted. But as I mentioned earlier, it took me twenty years to figure it out if I didn't exercise, my depression deepened. This only added to my stress because my responsibilities didn't stop. When you are immobilized by depression, illness, foggy thinking and fatigue, taking care of business becomes even more stressful because everything is overwhelmingly difficult. You must move. Find something you enjoy. Don't worry about being the best, just do something physical for you alone. Things like walking, jogging, riding a bike, golf, tennis, gardening, yoga or any number of relatively easy work outs will have lasting effects on your mental health. Those muscles you have been neglecting may hurt for a few days, but you'll get through it. Once you do, you'll have one more thing to feel good about.

- **What are you putting in your mouth?** – Caretakers – another distinguishing characteristic of the codependent– are known for often neglecting themselves. They are too lost in their compassionate concern for others to worry about themselves or they are used to self-denial. Others purposely don't eat right because of a distorted self image and believe they are a lost cause anyway. Remember, fixing other people is much easier than looking in the mirror. The opposite extreme of this are the perfectionists who are constantly dieting in order to look like the ideal – and therefore acceptable- person they believe they should be but can never quite attain. This is also where bulimia, anorexia, extreme exercise programs and other dangerous habits are formed. What does your diet look like? Common sense tells us that if we eat healthy, nutritious food, we will be rewarded. If we live on processed, salty and fatty foods, we will pay. Silly as it may be to tell adults this, your body needs more than sodas, coffee and energy drinks when you're thirsty to stay healthy. Incorporate water into your routine – lots of it. Your body will function better, your teeth won't suffer from all the sugar and your skin will look more radiant. Make a decision to eat more fresh food. Vegetables and fruits that are in season are a delicious and rewarding alternative to a bag of chips. Ease up on the fatty meats. Replace empty carbs with whole grains. None of this is revolutionary but it amazes me how many people simply don't think about these things. Life is one gigantic, unhealthy habit. I've included a couple of my favorite cookbooks for some yummy recipes. Be willing to experiment!

- **Loosen up and play** –Many codependent people really aren't good at relaxing. It's work to play. It's easier to fix problems, worry, control everything, over-achieve and remain vigilant than it is to just lighten up and unwind. To get balance back in your life, stress has to be offset with relaxation. Otherwise the body will suffer. Give yourself permission to laugh and be carefree occasionally. Watch a funny movie, take a walk in a peaceful place or read a good book. Look in the mirror. Are there scowl lines? Is frowning your natural facial expression? A little thing like practicing how to smile – not just with your lips, but including your eyes, will automatically lighten your disposition. It's also a guaranteed way to get people to smile back. Decide to make some time for the things that take your mind off your stressors. This is not to be confused with numbing out with addictive activities such as too much television, over-eating, porn, drugs or booze. It's not unusual for individuals who come from highly stressful environments to have to learn how to play as part of ongoing therapy. Make the investment in yourself and re-educate your brain to enjoy life.

The body speaks – facing trauma

In Part One, I included Dr. Peter Levine's words regarding the effects that unresolved trauma can have on the body. It is time to consider that perhaps some, maybe even all of your physical problems may be rooted in trauma you have not come to terms with. Before you continue, I encourage you to reread the section on Trauma. See if any of it resonates with you.

Our bodies hold on to memories, even those our mind has forgotten or refuses to remember. The effects of and therapy for this phenomenon are the focus of an important clinical book, *Trauma and the Body* (Ogden, Minton, Pain, 2006). He writes:

"For the traumatized individual, the debilitating, repetitive cycle of interaction between mind and body keeps past traumas 'alive'.....many people are left with a fragmented memory of their traumatic experiences and a host of easily....reactivated responses...baffling, intense, nonverbal memories – sensorimotor (body related – JM) responses that 'tell the story' without words, *as though the body knows* (italics added)....they are often unaware that these reactions – intrusive body sensations, images, smells, physical pain and constriction, numbing and the inability to (control) arousal – are, in fact, remnants of past trauma."

The focus of this important work is a technique that incorporates therapeutic work with the body in addition to traditional talk therapy. This is known as **Somatic** (Greek for "of the body") **Therapy**. The founder of this groundbreaking work was none other than Dr. Peter Levine. His work is used all over the world to help survivors of rape, war, holocausts and severe accidents. It is only logical, then that the traumatic fallout for some codependents, which manifests in many ways, can also be addressed through this form of therapy.

To truly heal the mind, the effects of past trauma on the body must be addressed. Here is a synopsis of how somatic healing works, taken directly but with some simplification, from the same book noted earlier.

1. Client learns to regulate arousal by being given the resources needed to control defensive mechanisms in the body. This is called Dual Processing since awareness (mindfulness) of how the body responds is done simultaneously with talk therapy about the origins of the trauma.

2. Therapist 'tracks' the correlation of physical manifestations to what is being talked about and initiates experiments (exercises) to help the client learn how to tolerate somatic sensations while participating in traumatic memory until there is resolution (control, peace) in the body. *"Through mindfulness of present-moment organization of experience, the client shifts from being caught up in the story and upset*

about her reactions to becoming curious about them......
Clients do not get caught up in their trauma-related beliefs
or arousal, but, rather...study the body's responses." (Italics
added)

3. In time, those same tools are used to expand the client's
    capacity to engage more fully in daily life, develop intimate
    relationships, create new meanings and increase tolerance
    of positive effects.

This groundbreaking work may not be for everyone. Maybe
you didn't suffer an extreme traumatic event, just ongoing
dysfunction. But if you are one of the many who know
something happened that when focused on causes your body to
react in negative ways without your control, I hope you will
make an effort to find a qualified somatic therapist and commit
to the working through it. Testimonies of its effectiveness are
amazing.

Training for this work is extensive and is only available to
qualified professionals. In the Resource section I've included a
website you can go to for help finding one in your area. Rest
assured, in case this is a concern for you, there is little or no
actual physical touch or contact with the therapist. It is a safe and
proven way to work through physical aspects of your healing
process. If there isn't a therapist near you, learn all you can and
start understanding how your body and your thoughts are
triggering each other.

My oldest daughter has begun a career as a family and
marriage therapist. In her continual quest for the newest ways to
help clients recover, she has attended seminars by Dr. Levine, Pat
Ogden as well as others and introduced me to this fascinating area
of healing which I have continued to learn about. The process of
reading about this topic was not only eye-opening for me from a

research point of view, but also therapeutic. As I read the book mentioned above, I at last understood how my own experience, body and emotions were connected. It definitely brought up some powerful emotions and even physical sensations as I saw myself on those pages. I also learned how to monitor myself in new ways.

"All trauma is stressful, but not all stress is traumatic"[5]

If you're not struggling with the huge issue of trauma, but do suffer from physical issues related to ongoing stress such as general tightness, ongoing pain, bad posture, specific areas of weakness in the body or low energy, there are plenty of options for you. Healing massage can help. There are many varieties. Ask around - good chiropractors often know who the best massage therapists are - to find the kind that is focused on healing body work. Some prefer to work on sports injuries, others offer massage for relaxation. You are looking for one who has had the specific training to find those areas in your body that are out of alignment, overly stressed and in need of healing hands and strong intuition: an inner knowing where to put those therapeutic hands to do the most good. Regular exercise helps with these types of physical issues also, as do simple stretches, Pilates, yoga, Tai Chi and Qigong. All are aimed at bringing your focus inward with slow, deliberate moves designed to bring you mental peace as well as a more limber, healthy body.

Ultimately, the way you live will determine the health of your body, barring invasion of disease which is usually out of your control. Even then, if you look into it, you may find there are ways to slow down or reverse the effects. Take care of and nurture the body you've been given.

---

[5]   *Healing Trauma, Levine, 2008*

The basics most people learn as children are still true. Make sure you get regular, uninterrupted sleep. Incorporate some kind of exercise into your life which you find enjoyable. Don't try running if you have bad knees; it'll only give you a reason to give up. Just do something that keeps your body in motion. It will help your brain, heart, emotions and every other aspect of your being to stay in harmony. Having a partner may help keep your enthusiasm alive.

Eat right. I know it's fun to eat whatever we like (or are used to). But I'm asking you to wake and to *be aware* of what you're putting in your mouth and begin to connect with how it's making you feel.

Finally, start using your own inner voice or intuition to listen to what is happening inside. Do this by being quiet for a moment and breathing. Pay attention to yourself. Codependent people often neglect warning signs then fall apart. You don't have to end up in that position.

Go back to the beginning of this section and review the main physical issues you described. Can you identify a relationship between stress and harmful habits that may be contributing to your problems?

For instance, skin allergies are often related to stress as are digestive issues. Stress has also been linked to more serious, deteriorating disease besides cancer such as Parkinson's. Take an honest inventory of your health and see where everything we've addressed here could make a positive difference.

By utilizing the information in this section, you can create a sense of being physically grounded and whole. It's what you were meant to have all along.

Summary on the body

- Decide to take an honest look at how healthy you really are.
- Remember this isn't about how attractive you can look; it's

about your well-being.
- If trauma is part of your story find professional help to overcome the effects it is taking on your body.
- Address areas of discomfort caused by stress in your body and work on them.
- Incorporate better eating habits, regular exercise and adequate rest into your schedule.
- Accept the fact that unresolved stress can lead to deadly disease and premature aging.
- Listen to your inner voice, your intuition, which tells you when your body is in need of attention.
- Respect your physical self. Learn to see your body as worth taking care of. It is never too late.
- Be willing to take responsibility for your own health.

SECTION FOUR

YOUR SOUL

"Diseases of the soul are more dangerous and more numerous than those of the body" – Cicero

"Be anxious for nothing, but in everything by prayer and supplication with thanksgiving let your requests be made known to God." – Philippians 4:6

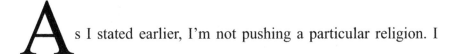

A s I stated earlier, I'm not pushing a particular religion. I don't even care for the term, 'religion' because in my estimation most of it is man-made. Rather than seek out a religion, I encourage you to instead to pursue a personal relationship with God (Creator, Higher Power).

The important point and the entire reason for this section is this: not believing there is a higher power available to help you get through the hardships in your life is a terrible, lonely burden to put on yourself.

Going back to the concept of holistic health, remember it's a triad: body, mind and soul (spirit). We've addressed the mind and the body. I would not be completing the job of giving you the tools to overcome codependency if I didn't talk about how absolutely important the spiritual aspect of the journey to healing is. And as I said from the beginning, all I can talk about with authority is what worked for me.

The battle position – on your knees

If you believe light exists, you must acknowledge that darkness does, too. In the same sense, if you are willing to believe there is a God, or goodness in the world, then you must face the fact evil is here as well.

You have an enemy. This enemy does not want you to be stable, calm, happy, strong or filled with 'the peace that passes all understanding.' Consequently, when you start being mindful of your progress, you'll start noticing every time you move forward in one area of your life, suddenly new challenges, roadblocks and little annoying hindrances will pop up all over. This isn't random; it is by design.

By being aware, you have the new responsibility of thwarting these attempts to steal your joy and your growth. You can't do this if you don't know what you believe in.

I was just like a lot of other lazy Christians. I thought if I went to church once a week and got my ticket punched, I had done my part. Then I got mad when God didn't appear in an apparition to change my circumstances. Being a seriously committed codependent, I really thought I could control my surroundings and fix everything and everyone on my own. Of course, things just got worse.

Like every family, we had problems. The stress level was always pretty high even in the good times due to certain factors. But it wasn't until my youngest daughter got lost in the dark world of drugs and all the ugliness that went with it that I found myself on my knees, sobbing to God for help repeatedly.

I got serious about my prayer. I sought out people who were much further along in their spiritual growth who could support me in my efforts to find connection with and help from God. In the process I read many books, especially the Bible; listened to many different teachers, sought out a good church and prayed. I prayed and prayed and prayed. I also kept journals which is how I can recall so many details about this period in our lives.

Every time it seemed our prayers had been answered, the 'problem' seemed to morph into something different and bigger. I felt hopeless repeatedly, but even when I was fed up and truly wanted to quit, I knew that if I – this girl's mother – gave up on her, no one else would be there. She had done a pretty thorough job of wearing everyone out, including me. Still, I knew I had to hang in there for her sake, but I needed help.

I don't remember when the true breaking point came – it seemed like there was one every week – but the time came when I finally realized all I could do was turn her over to God.

Even though I had spoken those words over and over before, I hadn't really done it. I was still frantically trying everything to save her, fix the problem and get my daughter back. Nothing worked.

Her story is a complex one and I'm so happy to say that as of this writing, it is moving in the right direction. She has taught me, by dedicating herself to her own sobriety through AA that life really does have to be taken one day at a time. So I'm learning to do the same.

But there was a five year stretch of time when I was constantly crying, praying and stressing. At least I was spending a lot of time with God. Because of that, I saw many miraculous changes I know would not have been possible had I not asked. Our daughter became committed to prayer as well and learned to depend on God. She would fall away and then return, just as I had, when things got tough. As I got stronger in my walk with God, I gradually got comfortable talking about it with both my daughters and I believe it's one of the main reasons we are so close today.

Not surprisingly, as our situation gradually got better I got lazier about praying. I had to remind myself to stay strong in my belief. Then some dip in the road would come along and I'd be on my knees again.

I am not the same person I was before all this happened. Aside from working on issues related to codependency, I have developed a much closer relationship with God in large part because of our trials with our daughter.

In doing so, I've had to make some changes. It meant letting some people go out of my life because they were pulling me in a direction contrary to where I wanted to be. I began seeing the world through wiser, more compassionate eyes. I felt calmer inside. I stopped being so hard on myself and realized that God was doing work in me for the better. It became easier for me not to worry, obsess and reason. Instead, I'd take a breath, say a little prayer asking for guidance or help and remind myself to trust.

Allowing God to be in my moment to moment existence has changed my life. *That happened when I literally fell to my knees and asked for help.*

Codependent people are constantly in a power struggle between themselves and everybody else, including God. The belief that we can handle whatever comes along makes us our own worst enemy in letting God in our lives. It often takes a broken spirit before we see that we are powerless and let our higher power take over. It is the basis of the Twelve Step Program because it is a proven, foundational truth.

Once you understand you can do nothing without God's help it becomes easy to see, in retrospect, why so many parts of your life just aren't working. Just as in the piece about delegating in the previous section, we don't even think to ask for God's help until it's almost too late. We're programmed to take everything on alone because we don't know the depth of our own weaknesses. Our capacity for suffering is enormous.

The good news is when we do finally throw our hands up, fall on our knees and cry out for help, He is always there. You just have to get to the point where you can trust the concept. *That means having faith.*

This is particularly hard for us because trust doesn't come easy if at all. What if we trust and nothing changes? That could happen. The tough part about recognizing a higher power is He uses His own timeline, not yours. Many people in the Bible believed for things their whole lives and died without ever seeing them come to pass. Yet they never stopped having faith; eventually, all they believed for did occur - in God's perfect timing.

Being controlling is the opposite of having faith

So how does all this fit into your plan to overcome codependency? It requires you to give up the thing that most defines who you are: control – the opposite of having faith.

Throughout this Guide, I have written about the benefits of being mindful. This simply means developing an awareness of how you think and function both mentally and physically. To develop your spiritual muscle, think of taking that mindfulness to a higher level. This means becoming aware not just of yourself, but the presence of God in your life. In reality, He's always there, but so often we just forget or worse, make a decision to ignore His presence. Our fear of abandonment need not exist with our

---

Vital Sign

"The thief comes only to steal, kill and destroy; I came that they might have life, and *might have it abundantly* " John10:10

Heavenly Father.

By becoming aware of a loving God in your life, you instantly seize upon a new source of strength. This strength will help and guide you through all the challenges you face including loneliness, fear, loss or pain.

Every goal or suggestion I've put forth in this book will be easier and within your reach with God's help. All you have to do is accept it. It's possible you don't think you are worthy of such goodness. If that's got you stuck, please go back and read **Truth #4.**

Simple truths

Here are some simple truths to help bring home the concept of allowing God in your life. They've helped change my life. I believe they will help you, too.

- Those things you were forced to live with as a child that stole your innocence, put too much responsibility on you and warped your personal values were caused
  by people who were separated from God.

- You have within you everything you need to stop bad habits, start good ones and have the life
  you want, with help from your higher power.

- There is no one you need approval from,
  and nothing you need to prove.

- You only answer to a loving Creator.

- As discussed earlier, when you wander away and do things which cause you to have remorse and shame, you don't have to carry it around forever. Asking God once with sincerity for forgiveness – and receiving
  it - is all that's required to be set free.

- You will have bad days. Ask for help.
  He is always with you.

- You really can do all things through
  Him who lives in you.

- Once you incorporate God in your life, you will
  start seeing the world differently and even better,
  the world will begin seeing *you* differently.

- There is no power in being passive or procrastinating.
  God meets us when we do all we can. He will do the rest.

- Miracles happen all the time.
  You just haven't been aware until now.

- Some prayers are answered immediately
  and it's awesome.

- Nothing is too small or too great to talk to God about.

- God does not remember our wrong doing. When we
  obsess about it, we give our power away.

- You are not an accident or a mistake. You are a child of
  God and you are loved....you always have been.

I believe we all have to deal with an adversary who does not want us to have the good life God intended for us to have. He will look for openings in your thoughts, your body and your spiritual life.

But you also have an omnipotent power on your side that will provide what you need when you need it. Ask for help and guidance. Be aware. Don't let yourself be victimized at every turn. Know that every time you show strength, you will come up against another challenge. That's how it works. But good does win over evil for those who persevere.

In closing of this section, I want to reiterate: I am not writing this book to convert anyone. I share what worked for me (and continues to.) **If reading about God offends you, there are other resources that may help you**. Check with your local hospitals for support groups that don't include faith in a higher power. There are books and websites that offer resources. It is my fervent belief, however, that choosing to handle life and all its problems by yourself is a lonely, harder way to go. Nevertheless, I wish you well.

Summary on the soul

- You have an enemy who does not want you to be well or happy.
- You also have God on your side. Ask for His help!
- Anything is possible for those who believe.
- You are loved just as you are and always have been by God.
- Leave revenge, punishment and justice to Him.
- Bad things will happen. Remain faithful and strong.

SECTION FIVE

YOUR ENVIRONMENT

"An unexamined life is not worth living." – Socrates

W hat we surround ourselves with is a pretty good indicator of our state of mind. Look around. What does your lifestyle and environment say about you? In this final section, we're going to take a brief look at several areas of your life that may need to be cleaned up or replaced. You've made a huge commitment to become a healthier person. You can't maintain momentum if you are surrounded by things and people that don't support your effort or worse, detract or steal your energy from it.

People – You'll find as you develop boundaries and positive habits, a few people in your life are not going to want you to get healthy. Or they may be lost in their own story, filled with negativity and wanting similar company. Writer and life coach Martha Beck addresses this crossroads in her book, *Steering by Starlight*. "When you dissolve the false beliefs that held you prisoner, people around you can't stay connected with both the New You and their old patterns of behavior." She goes on to explain a phase we go through when this happens. She calls it "The empty elevator." In essence, as you evolve people who could only relate to your old circumstances and behavior will eventually get off the elevator and you will go through a period of feeling alone.

The good news is that as you walk out into the world consistently living in the healthy ways you've worked so hard to achieve, you'll slowly start attracting like-minded, healthier, new people into your life.

This 'alone' phase is a valuable time for you. Learn to enjoy being by yourself. Part of getting healthy, as we talked about in the section about Boundaries, is you do not need to be with people all the time so you can be showered with affirmations. The stronger you become, the more relaxed you are with being alone.

If you are in a relationship with someone who is battling addiction and you are committed to being sober, you have a tough decision to make. If you are finding solace in a relationship with God and you are spending time with people who live in ungodly ways, such as hurting others, not living with integrity, or whose beliefs run contrary to your own, you are going to feel a tug.

As with every other aspect of your life, listen to your inner voice. Be mindful of who you are spending your time with. It's wonderful that you can now be a good influence on someone else, but you cannot let other people continue to be a bad influence on you.

Clean house – One of the off-shoots of problems like depression, fatigue, anxiety and constant busy-ness in other people's affairs is we can let our own little world get cluttered until we feel overwhelmed. What is your environment conveying

Vital Sign

"The secret of health for both mind and body is not to mourn for the past, worry about the future or anticipate troubles; but to live in the present moment wisely and earnestly." – Buddha

to the world? If it's: "I am a mess. My life is a wreck. It's hopeless" then take an honest look at why you create the surroundings you do. My suggestion is to clean house. Start getting rid of stuff. If you don't need it, can't wear it or don't have room for it; donate it. Your environment is a true mirror of your inner state. The sense of a weight being lifted of your shoulders is incredibly refreshing.

Once you can see the walls and floors again, start tidying up. Don't get anal about trying to make it perfect. We aren't concerned with that, only manageability, remember? Get your home opened up and aired out. If that's asking too much, pick one project. For instance, clear off your desk. File those papers and put the junk away. Then sit down, have a cup of tea and enjoy it. A couple hours of physical labor will provide a calm, pleasant environment you can actually relax in. Your old buddies – shame and guilt - will be replaced, for a while anyway, with healthy pride. Letting the light into the corners of your world is about exposing lies in the mind, but it is also has a very down to earth physical reward, too. Remember: you are worthy of beauty and calm.

What kind of music do you listen to? If you're still singing along to sad songs about heartbreak and misery, stop. Find something uplifting that makes you smile. Be more aware of what you're watching on tv or at the movies. If they are full of dysfunction, violence and tension, stop. Make a conscious decision to only fill your mind with positive, uplifting or humorous entertainment. If you are a cynical, anxious wreck, stop watching the news 24/7. These changes may seem unimportant to you, but every thought, sound and image you take in is influencing your mind and emotions either positively or negatively on some level.

Finances – A major problem people lose sleep over is

money. When we live beyond our means, don't pay bills on time and never have enough money; there can be no peace and that is the goal in your life. In order to have it, one of the things you must face is your finances. If you're behind in payments, face reality, talk to the right people and make arrangements. Stop using your charge card. Learn to live with what you can afford. It may feel like a huge sacrifice for a while, but the end result will be self- respect where fear and anxiety used to be. Your loved ones will be relieved that you are not venting your frustrations on them any- more, too. Having financial control is liberating and creates a sense of inner strength. Try it. You are worthy of financial security.

Your world view – Ever notice how you don't notice Volkswagens until you decide to buy one? Then they're everywhere. The same is true in life. If all you focus on is the negative, that's all you will see. Conversely, if you train yourself to look for the good, you will see things others don't.

For example, yesterday it rained most of the day. I found the lightning, thunder, wind and straight sheets of rain comforting as I wrote. Later, the sun came out. I was driving down our road, being mindful of my breathing because I was going to my mother's and I wanted to be calm. I happened to see a young girl on roller blades. Her light brown hair was gently swaying in the wind as she glided down the sidewalk. She had a bright red daisy tucked behind one ear and in her hand was a bunch of colorful wild flowers. It was such a lovely sight. It made me happy. It gave me hope. I don't know why. But I do know that if I wasn't 'awake' enough to look for the beauty in the world, all I would have seen was the muddy road ahead as my body tensed up, preparing for my daily visit with mom.

My new habit of purposefully looking for good made the difference between having a sweet moment or an ordinary one. Be fully awake in your world. Take off those negative lenses you've been seeing the world through. Be mindful of what you are thinking about and how you interpret events throughout your day. Make a decision that you are going to be at peace and remind yourself to correct your thinking when it reverts back to habitual negativity.

Reinforcements - If you don't already have some, you will need reinforcements. Find a God-centered church or temple. Not for the rules and legalism but to meet like-minded people who want to live in peace. You may have to shop around for a while until you find the right fit, but it will be worth it. Don't give up. When you're ready, make an effort to slowly get involved with people and groups that support your lifestyle. If you need to join organizations like AA or ACA (for adult children of alcoholics) or Celebrate Recovery (a Christ-centered form of AA) to help you stay on track, don't put it off. Having support is one of the most important pillars of success for the overcomer. Information is provided in the Resource section to help you.

On the flip side, you will need to stop going to places that work against you. As they say in AA, according to my daughter, "If you go to a barbershop often enough, eventually you're going to get a haircut." Such truth!

You can't continue bar hopping with your old friends if drinking is a problem for you. But as you grow into your new life, you won't have to be told this. The inner voice you have will be steering you, if you listen. You won't want to sit for hours and gossip or complain with other miserable people. It will feel all wrong. Congratulations, you are making progress!

Seek out positive role models. Maybe you aren't a good conversationalist; watch the ones in a crowd who are and learn from them. Maybe you feel like an old grouch who doesn't know how to have fun. Do you have difficulty making new friends?

Observe others who have those gifts and watch; learn –emulate.

Your personal impact – Every time you open your mouth or take action -or do not- you are impacting the world around you. Your words have power. Not just in your own head but in the minds of others who hear them. Are you speaking in a way to inspire and encourage those you touch or are you still letting negative thoughts fall out of your mouth with no concern as to how they might affect others? Is the way you present yourself sending a message that is congruent with the type of person you are working so hard to be? Ladies, are you still dressing too provocatively for the type of person you aspire to become? If so, remind yourself when you look in the mirror that your worth no longer comes from getting stared at. Are you walking with grace or schlepping around oblivious as to how you are coming across? In the codependents' mindset, being frantic, stressed and frazzled is somehow twisted into being a good thing. It is not. Your aim – by taking on all this book offers – is to acquire the skills to present yourself as balanced and appropriately aware of yourself. It's a big undertaking but well worth it. It also takes away from any temptation you might still have to go fix someone else instead.

The inner universe – The state of your environment originates with your beliefs. You have read the word 'mindful' at least fifty times in the course of this book. That was by design. It is the single most important nugget of information I hope stays with you. What you think about will determine how you feel, how you behave and your health to a great degree. Are you still obsessing? Do you allow yourself to be judgmental of every person you come in contact with in a negative way? Are you living in fear or are you turning toward having faith? To change how you think you're going to have to start by taking each thought captive, as it says in the Bible, which may have been one of the best descriptions of mindfulness ever. You must be vigilant in your awareness as to what you let yourself think about. When you find you're back to negative thinking, use your new-found awareness to turn it around. If you're struggling, refer back to the first section of this Guide which talks about mindfulness. Develop the habit of praying. There isn't one perfect manner in which to do it. Just talk to God. A great way to start is to give thanks. It will help you remember the good things in your life. When you're walking, working, laying in bed, driving, or whenever you need to talk, just do it. Don't be concerned with the sophistication of it. No one is listening but God. If you've spent your life talking about your problems, it's going to be challenging to speak positively. There is nothing wrong with just listening until you have something positive to offer. Happy, well-adjusted people are attracted to happy, well-adjusted people. Be ever mindful of what is about to come out of your mouth.

Your environment is a reflection of how you feel about yourself. Look around occasionally and do take a mental inventory. Now and then, you'll see some area in need of your attention.

Summary on your environment

- As you grow you will go through a period of being lonely as people who cannot or will not relate to the new you fall away. Use this time to get comfortable with yourself. New friends are on the way.
- Do an inventory of your environment. From time to time you will have to 'clean house,' make improvements and changes to reflect a healthier you.
- Be aware of how you impact the world around you and the messages you are putting out to people by the way you dress, talk, behave.
- Seek out a support system.
- Be ever mindful of your thinking. It is the source of everything

you create in your world.

- Having faith in a higher power will be the source of your strength when everything else falls away, if you allow yourself this gift in your life.

CONCLUSION

"I have set before you life and death; the blessing and the curse. So choose life in order that you may live; you and your descendants." – God

At the beginning of this Guide, I asked you to see yourself from a new perspective. By making this commitment, you will see slow but steady progress. Don't be hard on yourself because you stumble. That's all part of it. Just get up and keep going.

I challenge you to keep this book which hopefully is full of your words and not just mine. Make a note to check back in six months or a year to see how far you've come. I've had jaw-dropping moments when I've done this with journals and books I've used. *By having a gauge to actually see your progress as well as where you are still stuck, you can celebrate your growth and renew your efforts in areas you need to work on.*

You and I will always be a work in progress. As my hero, Joyce Meyer likes to say, "I may not have had a good start, but I'm going to have a great finish!" I whole heartedly embrace that mentality. I hope you will, too.

Finally, I ask you to do one last, very important thing. Be grateful. You are fortunate because you have decided to break through the lies you've been force-fed and grasped the belief that you can have a good life. You are worthy. In spite of whatever happened, you are a good person. Even if it hasn't happened yet, keep your faith strong that what you earnestly believe for is on its way. It's easy to forget how we've been blessed when we're always crying out for more.

As I write this, someone I care about has lost her valiant two- year battle with cancer. This is a person who was accustomed to taking life by the horns and getting things done. But in spite of her determination, she will not see another Christmas or celebrate another birthday. When I think of her, I am overcome with the raw truth that I am blessed beyond my own comprehension by just having my health. Sensing the clock ticking for someone else these last two years has made me even more determined to live each day to the fullest. Writing this book is a big part of my goal to live my life to the best of my ability by helping others.

Codependency is only dangerous if you don't understand it. Now you do and it no longer has to define who you are. You are not crazy; you have been fighting an invisible enemy. Now it has been exposed. It is my prayer that in reading it, you've gained new clarity, tools and inspiration to do whatever is required to live *your* best life.

The ripple effects of the hard work you are undertaking now will have a positive impact not only on everyone whose lives you touch now, *but on your family for generations to come.* That's an awesome promise and God doesn't lie.

* * *

EPILOGUE

Everything I have experienced starting with my sick family of origin to the trials of dealing with the addiction and related problems of my youngest daughter and all that happened in between have made me stronger in ways I could never have imagined just because I didn't let the hurdles I had to overcome defeat me, even though I did feel like I was losing my mind many times. Codependency has been the hardest problem to overcome because it is so elusive and hard to recognize. Those of us who have had to work through it know that when you think you've overcome one area, it shows up in another. Codependency is a ruthless enemy, but not invincible.

I am not the same person I was two years ago, let alone twenty or forty. I have come through what many have: the tunnel of depression, hopelessness, fear, loss of self, insecurity, endless worry and most of all the terrifying knowledge I was on the brink of passing all that on to my beautiful daughters.

If you don't get anything else, remember this: On the other side of that tunnel are strength, peace and well-being if you don't give up.

The secret weapon, as Mark Twain's quote alluded to at the beginning of this book, is not to avoid fear but to do whatever must be done even though we feel afraid. Being fearless can be scary. Do it anyway.

We've covered a lot of serious, important ground here. It's easy to forget to laugh at ourselves and at life. Yes, you have stuff to work through, but keeping a sense of humor will help. One of the best things a codependent person can do is learn not to take themselves quite so seriously. With that in mind, I leave you with a lighthearted quote:

You're Not Crazy-You're Codependent

"It's ok to be crazy, just don't let it drive you nuts." – Jimmy Buffet

"Thank you for reading my book. I'm humbled that you've chosen it to help you on your journey of healing. I hope you did the work and found it helpful. I welcome your comments. Feel free to contact me at: jeanettementer@gmail.com. "

175

RESOURCES

The information I have included here are some of my personal favorites as well as a few basic resources I hope you will find helpful.

Mindfulness

www.eomega.org
Website for Jon Kabat-Zinn, PhD
Here, you can read all about mindfulness and
search for a practitioner.

www.plumvillage.org
Official site for Buddhist monk and spiritual teacher
on Mindfulness, Thich Nhat Hanh.
Lots of ideas for creating a simpler, peaceful life.

www.mbct.com
Another good site to get additional information on
mindfulness and how it is used to combat depression.

Somatic Therapy

www.traumahealing.com
Here you will find everything you need to know about
somatic healing and information about the work being done at
the Somatic Experiencing Trauma Institute, led by Dr. Peter
Levine. You can also search for a practitioner.

Addiction
www.AA.org
The official site for Alcoholics Anonymous
with resources of every kind.

www.adultchildren.org (ACA)
For people who grew up with someone
who was involved with addiction

www.alanon.org
For friends and families of problem drinkers

www.alanon.alateen.org
Specializing in problems with teen chemical dependency

www.NA.org (Narcotics Anonymous)
For drugs other than alcohol

CelebrateRecovery.com
National organization offering meetings and resources for
Christians struggling with addiction

*"The Addictive Personality –
Understanding the Addictive Process
and Compulsive Behavior"*
Craig Nakken
An excellent book that covers the process
of addiction, reasons and recovery.

Shame
"Bradshaw On: The Family"
John Bradshaw
An amazing exploration into the family dynamic
and some of the toxic shame-based effects it has on children.

Abuse
"Healing Trauma"
Peter A. Levine, Ph.D.
Powerful book which explains the effects of trauma on the body
and exercises to help overcome those effects.
Comes with an accompanying CD.

"The Courage to Heal"
Laura Davis
Specifically written for men and women of childhood sexual
abuse. There is also an accompanying workbook available.

"Trauma and the Body"
Pat Ogden, Kekuni Minton, Clare Pain
This is a clinical textbook and is geared towards professionals.
It provides technical, fascinating insight into the area of
Somatic Therapy for dealing with trauma and abuse.

"Healing the Wounds of Abuse – A Manual for Self Help"
Paul C. Liederman, M.D. & Farideh H. Resai, PhD.
A little known book given to me in 1992 by a counselor.
Addresses the effects of child abuse and ways to heal from it.

Spiritual direction
"The Bible"
There are hundreds of versions. "The Life Recovery Bible –
New Living Translation" is excellent for those committed to
overcoming addiction and developing healthy lives/choices.

"The Screwtape Letters"
C.S. Lewis
Described as, "A devil's diabolical advice for
the capturing of the human heart"
This little book gives excellent examples of how our 'enemy' is
always working against us in ways we never even notice.
(Anything by C.S. Lewis is worth reading)

"The Case for Faith"
Lee Strobel
Another atheist turned Christian writes about his journey.

"Your God Is Too Small"
J.B. Phillips
Written by a minister who reminds us
that God can do much more
than we give Him credit for.

"Battlefield of the Mind"
Joyce Meyer
A great Christian-based book on wrong thinking and bad
attitudes and how to change them. An important book
for anyone to read.
Her website www.joycemeyer.org
offers an abundance of resources

Finding your purpose
"Steering by Starlight"
Martha Beck
One of the most inspiring books I've ever read.

"A New Earth – Awakening to Your Life's Purpose"
Eckhart Tolle
The title says it all. Tolle talks not just about transcending
our ego-centered lives to find happiness, but takes
his ideas to the global level for a better life.

"A Case for Christian Faith"
C.S. Lewis
A pragmatic approach to understanding the value and truth
of Christianity.

"To Be Told"
Dan B. Allender, PhD.
Book and Workbook to help you 'co-author' your life by asking
questions which when answered in a journaling format, help
you create the life you've always wanted. Christian-based.

Physical wellbeing
"Perfect Health – A Complete Mind Body Guide"
Deepak Chopra, M.D.

"Stress Less"
Don Colbert, M.D.
Addresses how worry, fear and other negative habits affect the
body and how to deal with them. Christian-based.

*"The Way of Qigong – The Art and Science of
Chinese Energy Healing"*
Kenneth S. Cohen
If you're looking for a new way to get a physical workout
that also provides mental and spiritual nurturing,
this book shows how and why to do it.

www.healthjourneys.com
One of my favorite places to find all sorts of CD's
and other tools to help you relax, meditate and create good
thinking and breathing habits. Offers help and
healing for a multitude of issues.

*"The Life-Changing Magic of Tidying Up: The Japanese Art
of Decluterring and Organizing"*
Marie Kondo
The best-seller for those who need guidance and inspiration
to make their environments less messy

Eating well
"The Sonoma Diet"
Dr. Connie Guttersen, Ph.D.
Not so much a diet as a healthier, tasty way to eat well
while being good to your body. Note: This program isn't for
everybody as it does allow for limited consumption of wine.

"The South Beach Diet Cookbook"
Arthur Agatston, M.D.
Based on sound nutritional principals,
it offers interesting, healthy recipes.

NEVER GIVE UP ON LEARNING TO LOVE YOURSELF

You're Not Crazy-You're Codependent